C-189 CAREER EXAMINATION SERIES

This is your
PASSBOOK for...

Chief Clerk

Test Preparation Study Guide
Questions & Answers

NATIONAL LEARNING CORPORATION®

COPYRIGHT NOTICE

This book is SOLELY intended for, is sold ONLY to, and its use is RESTRICTED to individual, bona fide applicants or candidates who qualify by virtue of having seriously filed applications for appropriate license, certificate, professional and/or promotional advancement, higher school matriculation, scholarship, or other legitimate requirements of education and/or governmental authorities.

This book is NOT intended for use, class instruction, tutoring, training, duplication, copying, reprinting, excerption, or adaptation, etc., by:

1) Other publishers
2) Proprietors and/or Instructors of "Coaching" and/or Preparatory Courses
3) Personnel and/or Training Divisions of commercial, industrial, and governmental organizations
4) Schools, colleges, or universities and/or their departments and staffs, including teachers and other personnel
5) Testing Agencies or Bureaus
6) Study groups which seek by the purchase of a single volume to copy and/or duplicate and/or adapt this material for use by the group as a whole without having purchased individual volumes for each of the members of the group
7) Et al.

Such persons would be in violation of appropriate Federal and State statutes.

PROVISION OF LICENSING AGREEMENTS – Recognized educational, commercial, industrial, and governmental institutions and organizations, and others legitimately engaged in educational pursuits, including training, testing, and measurement activities, may address request for a licensing agreement to the copyright owners, who will determine whether, and under what conditions, including fees and charges, the materials in this book may be used them. In other words, a licensing facility exists for the legitimate use of the material in this book on other than an individual basis. However, it is asseverated and affirmed here that the material in this book CANNOT be used without the receipt of the express permission of such a licensing agreement from the Publishers. Inquiries re licensing should be addressed to the company, attention rights and permissions department.

All rights reserved, including the right of reproduction in whole or in part, in any form or by any means, electronic or mechanical, including photocopying, recording, or by any information storage and retrieval system, without permission in writing from the Publisher.

Copyright © 2025 by
National Learning Corporation

212 Michael Drive, Syosset, NY 11791
(516) 921-8888 • www.passbooks.com
E-mail: info@passbooks.com

PASSBOOK® SERIES

THE *PASSBOOK® SERIES* has been created to prepare applicants and candidates for the ultimate academic battlefield – the examination room.

At some time in our lives, each and every one of us may be required to take an examination – for validation, matriculation, admission, qualification, registration, certification, or licensure.

Based on the assumption that every applicant or candidate has met the basic formal educational standards, has taken the required number of courses, and read the necessary texts, the *PASSBOOK® SERIES* furnishes the one special preparation which may assure passing with confidence, instead of failing with insecurity. Examination questions – together with answers – are furnished as the basic vehicle for study so that the mysteries of the examination and its compounding difficulties may be eliminated or diminished by a sure method.

This book is meant to help you pass your examination provided that you qualify and are serious in your objective.

The entire field is reviewed through the huge store of content information which is succinctly presented through a provocative and challenging approach – the question-and-answer method.

A climate of success is established by furnishing the correct answers at the end of each test.

You soon learn to recognize types of questions, forms of questions, and patterns of questioning. You may even begin to anticipate expected outcomes.

You perceive that many questions are repeated or adapted so that you can gain acute insights, which may enable you to score many sure points.

You learn how to confront new questions, or types of questions, and to attack them confidently and work out the correct answers.

You note objectives and emphases, and recognize pitfalls and dangers, so that you may make positive educational adjustments.

Moreover, you are kept fully informed in relation to new concepts, methods, practices, and directions in the field.

You discover that you are actually taking the examination all the time: you are preparing for the examination by "taking" an examination, not by reading extraneous and/or supererogatory textbooks.

In short, this PASSBOOK®, used directedly, should be an important factor in helping you to pass your test.

CHIEF CLERK

DUTIES
In charge of clerks in a bureau or office. Performs highly difficult, complex, and responsible clerical functions which may involve supervision over a large number of subordinate personnel. Performs related work as required.

SCOPE OF THE WRITTEN TEST
The written test will be designed to cover knowledges, skills, and/or abilities in the following areas:
1. Office and secretarial practices;
2. Public and interpersonal relations;
3. Preparation of written material;
4. Reading comprehension;
5. Arithmetic reasoning;
6. Supervision; and
7. Administration.

HOW TO TAKE A TEST

I. YOU MUST PASS AN EXAMINATION

A. *WHAT EVERY CANDIDATE SHOULD KNOW*

Examination applicants often ask us for help in preparing for the written test. What can I study in advance? What kinds of questions will be asked? How will the test be given? How will the papers be graded?

As an applicant for a civil service examination, you may be wondering about some of these things. Our purpose here is to suggest effective methods of advance study and to describe civil service examinations.

Your chances for success on this examination can be increased if you know how to prepare. Those "pre-examination jitters" can be reduced if you know what to expect. You can even experience an adventure in good citizenship if you know why civil service exams are given.

B. *WHY ARE CIVIL SERVICE EXAMINATIONS GIVEN?*

Civil service examinations are important to you in two ways. As a citizen, you want public jobs filled by employees who know how to do their work. As a job seeker, you want a fair chance to compete for that job on an equal footing with other candidates. The best-known means of accomplishing this two-fold goal is the competitive examination.

Exams are widely publicized throughout the nation. They may be administered for jobs in federal, state, city, municipal, town or village governments or agencies.

Any citizen may apply, with some limitations, such as the age or residence of applicants. Your experience and education may be reviewed to see whether you meet the requirements for the particular examination. When these requirements exist, they are reasonable and applied consistently to all applicants. Thus, a competitive examination may cause you some uneasiness now, but it is your privilege and safeguard.

C. *HOW ARE CIVIL SERVICE EXAMS DEVELOPED?*

Examinations are carefully written by trained technicians who are specialists in the field known as "psychological measurement," in consultation with recognized authorities in the field of work that the test will cover. These experts recommend the subject matter areas or skills to be tested; only those knowledges or skills important to your success on the job are included. The most reliable books and source materials available are used as references. Together, the experts and technicians judge the difficulty level of the questions.

Test technicians know how to phrase questions so that the problem is clearly stated. Their ethics do not permit "trick" or "catch" questions. Questions may have been tried out on sample groups, or subjected to statistical analysis, to determine their usefulness.

Written tests are often used in combination with performance tests, ratings of training and experience, and oral interviews. All of these measures combine to form the best-known means of finding the right person for the right job.

II. HOW TO PASS THE WRITTEN TEST

A. NATURE OF THE EXAMINATION

To prepare intelligently for civil service examinations, you should know how they differ from school examinations you have taken. In school you were assigned certain definite pages to read or subjects to cover. The examination questions were quite detailed and usually emphasized memory. Civil service exams, on the other hand, try to discover your present ability to perform the duties of a position, plus your potentiality to learn these duties. In other words, a civil service exam attempts to predict how successful you will be. Questions cover such a broad area that they cannot be as minute and detailed as school exam questions.

In the public service similar kinds of work, or positions, are grouped together in one "class." This process is known as *position-classification*. All the positions in a class are paid according to the salary range for that class. One class title covers all of these positions, and they are all tested by the same examination.

B. FOUR BASIC STEPS

1) Study the announcement

How, then, can you know what subjects to study? Our best answer is: "Learn as much as possible about the class of positions for which you've applied." The exam will test the knowledge, skills and abilities needed to do the work.

Your most valuable source of information about the position you want is the official exam announcement. This announcement lists the training and experience qualifications. Check these standards and apply only if you come reasonably close to meeting them.

The brief description of the position in the examination announcement offers some clues to the subjects which will be tested. Think about the job itself. Review the duties in your mind. Can you perform them, or are there some in which you are rusty? Fill in the blank spots in your preparation.

Many jurisdictions preview the written test in the exam announcement by including a section called "Knowledge and Abilities Required," "Scope of the Examination," or some similar heading. Here you will find out specifically what fields will be tested.

2) Review your own background

Once you learn in general what the position is all about, and what you need to know to do the work, ask yourself which subjects you already know fairly well and which need improvement. You may wonder whether to concentrate on improving your strong areas or on building some background in your fields of weakness. When the announcement has specified "some knowledge" or "considerable knowledge," or has used adjectives like "beginning principles of…" or "advanced … methods," you can get a clue as to the number and difficulty of questions to be asked in any given field. More questions, and hence broader coverage, would be included for those subjects which are more important in the work. Now weigh your strengths and weaknesses against the job requirements and prepare accordingly.

3) Determine the level of the position

Another way to tell how intensively you should prepare is to understand the level of the job for which you are applying. Is it the entering level? In other words, is this the position in which beginners in a field of work are hired? Or is it an intermediate or advanced level? Sometimes this is indicated by such words as "Junior" or "Senior" in the class title. Other jurisdictions use Roman numerals to designate the level – Clerk I, Clerk II, for example. The word "Supervisor" sometimes appears in the title. If the level is not indicated by the title, check the description of duties. Will you be working under very close supervision, or will you have responsibility for independent decisions in this work?

4) Choose appropriate study materials

Now that you know the subjects to be examined and the relative amount of each subject to be covered, you can choose suitable study materials. For beginning level jobs, or even advanced ones, if you have a pronounced weakness in some aspect of your training, read a modern, standard textbook in that field. Be sure it is up to date and has general coverage. Such books are normally available at your library, and the librarian will be glad to help you locate one. For entry-level positions, questions of appropriate difficulty are chosen – neither highly advanced questions, nor those too simple. Such questions require careful thought but not advanced training.

If the position for which you are applying is technical or advanced, you will read more advanced, specialized material. If you are already familiar with the basic principles of your field, elementary textbooks would waste your time. Concentrate on advanced textbooks and technical periodicals. Think through the concepts and review difficult problems in your field.

These are all general sources. You can get more ideas on your own initiative, following these leads. For example, training manuals and publications of the government agency which employs workers in your field can be useful, particularly for technical and professional positions. A letter or visit to the government department involved may result in more specific study suggestions, and certainly will provide you with a more definite idea of the exact nature of the position you are seeking.

III. KINDS OF TESTS

Tests are used for purposes other than measuring knowledge and ability to perform specified duties. For some positions, it is equally important to test ability to make adjustments to new situations or to profit from training. In others, basic mental abilities not dependent on information are essential. Questions which test these things may not appear as pertinent to the duties of the position as those which test for knowledge and information. Yet they are often highly important parts of a fair examination. For very general questions, it is almost impossible to help you direct your study efforts. What we can do is to point out some of the more common of these general abilities needed in public service positions and describe some typical questions.

1) General information

Broad, general information has been found useful for predicting job success in some kinds of work. This is tested in a variety of ways, from vocabulary lists to questions about current events. Basic background in some field of work, such as sociology or economics, may be sampled in a group of questions. Often these are principles which have become familiar to most persons through exposure rather than through formal training. It is difficult to advise you how to study for these questions; being alert to the world around you is our best suggestion.

2) Verbal ability

An example of an ability needed in many positions is verbal or language ability. Verbal ability is, in brief, the ability to use and understand words. Vocabulary and grammar tests are typical measures of this ability. Reading comprehension or paragraph interpretation questions are common in many kinds of civil service tests. You are given a paragraph of written material and asked to find its central meaning.

3) Numerical ability

Number skills can be tested by the familiar arithmetic problem, by checking paired lists of numbers to see which are alike and which are different, or by interpreting charts and graphs. In the latter test, a graph may be printed in the test booklet which you are asked to use as the basis for answering questions.

4) Observation

A popular test for law-enforcement positions is the observation test. A picture is shown to you for several minutes, then taken away. Questions about the picture test your ability to observe both details and larger elements.

5) Following directions

In many positions in the public service, the employee must be able to carry out written instructions dependably and accurately. You may be given a chart with several columns, each column listing a variety of information. The questions require you to carry out directions involving the information given in the chart.

6) Skills and aptitudes

Performance tests effectively measure some manual skills and aptitudes. When the skill is one in which you are trained, such as typing or shorthand, you can practice. These tests are often very much like those given in business school or high school courses. For many of the other skills and aptitudes, however, no short-time preparation can be made. Skills and abilities natural to you or that you have developed throughout your lifetime are being tested.

Many of the general questions just described provide all the data needed to answer the questions and ask you to use your reasoning ability to find the answers. Your best preparation for these tests, as well as for tests of facts and ideas, is to be at your physical and mental best. You, no doubt, have your own methods of getting into an exam-taking mood and keeping "in shape." The next section lists some ideas on this subject.

IV. KINDS OF QUESTIONS

Only rarely is the "essay" question, which you answer in narrative form, used in civil service tests. Civil service tests are usually of the short-answer type. Full instructions for answering these questions will be given to you at the examination. But in case this is your first experience with short-answer questions and separate answer sheets, here is what you need to know:

1) Multiple-choice Questions

Most popular of the short-answer questions is the "multiple choice" or "best answer" question. It can be used, for example, to test for factual knowledge, ability to solve problems or judgment in meeting situations found at work.

A multiple-choice question is normally one of three types—
- It can begin with an incomplete statement followed by several possible endings. You are to find the one ending which *best* completes the statement, although some of the others may not be entirely wrong.
- It can also be a complete statement in the form of a question which is answered by choosing one of the statements listed.

- It can be in the form of a problem – again you select the best answer.

Here is an example of a multiple-choice question with a discussion which should give you some clues as to the method for choosing the right answer:

When an employee has a complaint about his assignment, the action which will *best* help him overcome his difficulty is to
- A. discuss his difficulty with his coworkers
- B. take the problem to the head of the organization
- C. take the problem to the person who gave him the assignment
- D. say nothing to anyone about his complaint

In answering this question, you should study each of the choices to find which is best. Consider choice "A" – Certainly an employee may discuss his complaint with fellow employees, but no change or improvement can result, and the complaint remains unresolved. Choice "B" is a poor choice since the head of the organization probably does not know what assignment you have been given, and taking your problem to him is known as "going over the head" of the supervisor. The supervisor, or person who made the assignment, is the person who can clarify it or correct any injustice. Choice "C" is, therefore, correct. To say nothing, as in choice "D," is unwise. Supervisors have and interest in knowing the problems employees are facing, and the employee is seeking a solution to his problem.

2) True/False Questions

The "true/false" or "right/wrong" form of question is sometimes used. Here a complete statement is given. Your job is to decide whether the statement is right or wrong.

SAMPLE: A roaming cell-phone call to a nearby city costs less than a non-roaming call to a distant city.

This statement is wrong, or false, since roaming calls are more expensive.

This is not a complete list of all possible question forms, although most of the others are variations of these common types. You will always get complete directions for answering questions. Be sure you understand *how* to mark your answers – ask questions until you do.

V. RECORDING YOUR ANSWERS

Computer terminals are used more and more today for many different kinds of exams.

For an examination with very few applicants, you may be told to record your answers in the test booklet itself. Separate answer sheets are much more common. If this separate answer sheet is to be scored by machine – and this is often the case – it is highly important that you mark your answers correctly in order to get credit.

An electronic scoring machine is often used in civil service offices because of the speed with which papers can be scored. Machine-scored answer sheets must be marked with a pencil, which will be given to you. This pencil has a high graphite content which responds to the electronic scoring machine. As a matter of fact, stray dots may register as answers, so do not let your pencil rest on the answer sheet while you are pondering the correct answer. Also, if your pencil lead breaks or is otherwise defective, ask for another.

Since the answer sheet will be dropped in a slot in the scoring machine, be careful not to bend the corners or get the paper crumpled.

The answer sheet normally has five vertical columns of numbers, with 30 numbers to a column. These numbers correspond to the question numbers in your test booklet. After each number, going across the page are four or five pairs of dotted lines. These short dotted lines have small letters or numbers above them. The first two pairs may also have a "T" or "F" above the letters. This indicates that the first two pairs only are to be used if the questions are of the true-false type. If the questions are multiple choice, disregard the "T" and "F" and pay attention only to the small letters or numbers.

Answer your questions in the manner of the sample that follows:

32. The largest city in the United States is
    A. Washington, D.C.
    B. New York City
    C. Chicago
    D. Detroit
    E. San Francisco

1) Choose the answer you think is best. (New York City is the largest, so "B" is correct.)
2) Find the row of dotted lines numbered the same as the question you are answering. (Find row number 32)
3) Find the pair of dotted lines corresponding to the answer. (Find the pair of lines under the mark "B.")
4) Make a solid black mark between the dotted lines.

VI. BEFORE THE TEST

Common sense will help you find procedures to follow to get ready for an examination. Too many of us, however, overlook these sensible measures. Indeed, nervousness and fatigue have been found to be the most serious reasons why applicants fail to do their best on civil service tests. Here is a list of reminders:

- Begin your preparation early – Don't wait until the last minute to go scurrying around for books and materials or to find out what the position is all about.
- Prepare continuously – An hour a night for a week is better than an all-night cram session. This has been definitely established. What is more, a night a week for a month will return better dividends than crowding your study into a shorter period of time.
- Locate the place of the exam – You have been sent a notice telling you when and where to report for the examination. If the location is in a different town or otherwise unfamiliar to you, it would be well to inquire the best route and learn something about the building.
- Relax the night before the test – Allow your mind to rest. Do not study at all that night. Plan some mild recreation or diversion; then go to bed early and get a good night's sleep.
- Get up early enough to make a leisurely trip to the place for the test – This way unforeseen events, traffic snarls, unfamiliar buildings, etc. will not upset you.
- Dress comfortably – A written test is not a fashion show. You will be known by number and not by name, so wear something comfortable.

- Leave excess paraphernalia at home – Shopping bags and odd bundles will get in your way. You need bring only the items mentioned in the official notice you received; usually everything you need is provided. Do not bring reference books to the exam. They will only confuse those last minutes and be taken away from you when in the test room.
- Arrive somewhat ahead of time – If because of transportation schedules you must get there very early, bring a newspaper or magazine to take your mind off yourself while waiting.
- Locate the examination room – When you have found the proper room, you will be directed to the seat or part of the room where you will sit. Sometimes you are given a sheet of instructions to read while you are waiting. Do not fill out any forms until you are told to do so; just read them and be prepared.
- Relax and prepare to listen to the instructions
- If you have any physical problem that may keep you from doing your best, be sure to tell the test administrator. If you are sick or in poor health, you really cannot do your best on the exam. You can come back and take the test some other time.

VII. AT THE TEST

The day of the test is here and you have the test booklet in your hand. The temptation to get going is very strong. Caution! There is more to success than knowing the right answers. You must know how to identify your papers and understand variations in the type of short-answer question used in this particular examination. Follow these suggestions for maximum results from your efforts:

1) Cooperate with the monitor

The test administrator has a duty to create a situation in which you can be as much at ease as possible. He will give instructions, tell you when to begin, check to see that you are marking your answer sheet correctly, and so on. He is not there to guard you, although he will see that your competitors do not take unfair advantage. He wants to help you do your best.

2) Listen to all instructions

Don't jump the gun! Wait until you understand all directions. In most civil service tests you get more time than you need to answer the questions. So don't be in a hurry. Read each word of instructions until you clearly understand the meaning. Study the examples, listen to all announcements and follow directions. Ask questions if you do not understand what to do.

3) Identify your papers

Civil service exams are usually identified by number only. You will be assigned a number; you must not put your name on your test papers. Be sure to copy your number correctly. Since more than one exam may be given, copy your exact examination title.

4) Plan your time

Unless you are told that a test is a "speed" or "rate of work" test, speed itself is usually not important. Time enough to answer all the questions will be provided, but this does not mean that you have all day. An overall time limit has been set. Divide the total time (in minutes) by the number of questions to determine the approximate time you have for each question.

5) Do not linger over difficult questions

If you come across a difficult question, mark it with a paper clip (useful to have along) and come back to it when you have been through the booklet. One caution if you do this – be sure to skip a number on your answer sheet as well. Check often to be sure that you have not lost your place and that you are marking in the row numbered the same as the question you are answering.

6) Read the questions

Be sure you know what the question asks! Many capable people are unsuccessful because they failed to *read* the questions correctly.

7) Answer all questions

Unless you have been instructed that a penalty will be deducted for incorrect answers, it is better to guess than to omit a question.

8) Speed tests

It is often better NOT to guess on speed tests. It has been found that on timed tests people are tempted to spend the last few seconds before time is called in marking answers at random – without even reading them – in the hope of picking up a few extra points. To discourage this practice, the instructions may warn you that your score will be "corrected" for guessing. That is, a penalty will be applied. The incorrect answers will be deducted from the correct ones, or some other penalty formula will be used.

9) Review your answers

If you finish before time is called, go back to the questions you guessed or omitted to give them further thought. Review other answers if you have time.

10) Return your test materials

If you are ready to leave before others have finished or time is called, take ALL your materials to the monitor and leave quietly. Never take any test material with you. The monitor can discover whose papers are not complete, and taking a test booklet may be grounds for disqualification.

VIII. EXAMINATION TECHNIQUES

1) Read the general instructions carefully. These are usually printed on the first page of the exam booklet. As a rule, these instructions refer to the timing of the examination; the fact that you should not start work until the signal and must stop work at a signal, etc. If there are any *special* instructions, such as a choice of questions to be answered, make sure that you note this instruction carefully.

2) When you are ready to start work on the examination, that is as soon as the signal has been given, read the instructions to each question booklet, underline any key words or phrases, such as *least, best, outline, describe* and the like. In this way you will tend to answer as requested rather than discover on reviewing your paper that you *listed without describing*, that you selected the *worst* choice rather than the *best* choice, etc.

3) If the examination is of the objective or multiple-choice type – that is, each question will also give a series of possible answers: A, B, C or D, and you are called upon to select the best answer and write the letter next to that answer on your answer paper – it is advisable to start answering each question in turn. There may be anywhere from 50 to 100 such questions in the three or four hours allotted and you can see how much time would be taken if you read through all the questions before beginning to answer any. Furthermore, if you come across a question or group of questions which you know would be difficult to answer, it would undoubtedly affect your handling of all the other questions.

4) If the examination is of the essay type and contains but a few questions, it is a moot point as to whether you should read all the questions before starting to answer any one. Of course, if you are given a choice – say five out of seven and the like – then it is essential to read all the questions so you can eliminate the two that are most difficult. If, however, you are asked to answer all the questions, there may be danger in trying to answer the easiest one first because you may find that you will spend too much time on it. The best technique is to answer the first question, then proceed to the second, etc.

5) Time your answers. Before the exam begins, write down the time it started, then add the time allowed for the examination and write down the time it must be completed, then divide the time available somewhat as follows:
    - If 3-1/2 hours are allowed, that would be 210 minutes. If you have 80 objective-type questions, that would be an average of 2-1/2 minutes per question. Allow yourself no more than 2 minutes per question, or a total of 160 minutes, which will permit about 50 minutes to review.
    - If for the time allotment of 210 minutes there are 7 essay questions to answer, that would average about 30 minutes a question. Give yourself only 25 minutes per question so that you have about 35 minutes to review.

6) The most important instruction is to *read each question* and make sure you know what is wanted. The second most important instruction is to *time yourself properly* so that you answer every question. The third most important instruction is to *answer every question*. Guess if you have to but include something for each question. Remember that you will receive no credit for a blank and will probably receive some credit if you write something in answer to an essay question. If you guess a letter – say "B" for a multiple-choice question – you may have guessed right. If you leave a blank as an answer to a multiple-choice question, the examiners may respect your feelings but it will not add a point to your score. Some exams may penalize you for wrong answers, so in such cases *only*, you may not want to guess unless you have some basis for your answer.

7) Suggestions
    a. Objective-type questions
        1. Examine the question booklet for proper sequence of pages and questions
        2. Read all instructions carefully
        3. Skip any question which seems too difficult; return to it after all other questions have been answered
        4. Apportion your time properly; do not spend too much time on any single question or group of questions

5. Note and underline key words – *all, most, fewest, least, best, worst, same, opposite*, etc.
6. Pay particular attention to negatives
7. Note unusual option, e.g., unduly long, short, complex, different or similar in content to the body of the question
8. Observe the use of "hedging" words – *probably, may, most likely*, etc.
9. Make sure that your answer is put next to the same number as the question
10. Do not second-guess unless you have good reason to believe the second answer is definitely more correct
11. Cross out original answer if you decide another answer is more accurate; do not erase until you are ready to hand your paper in
12. Answer all questions; guess unless instructed otherwise
13. Leave time for review

  b. Essay questions
1. Read each question carefully
2. Determine exactly what is wanted. Underline key words or phrases.
3. Decide on outline or paragraph answer
4. Include many different points and elements unless asked to develop any one or two points or elements
5. Show impartiality by giving pros and cons unless directed to select one side only
6. Make and write down any assumptions you find necessary to answer the questions
7. Watch your English, grammar, punctuation and choice of words
8. Time your answers; don't crowd material

8) Answering the essay question

Most essay questions can be answered by framing the specific response around several key words or ideas. Here are a few such key words or ideas:

M's: manpower, materials, methods, money, management
P's: purpose, program, policy, plan, procedure, practice, problems, pitfalls, personnel, public relations

  a. Six basic steps in handling problems:
1. Preliminary plan and background development
2. Collect information, data and facts
3. Analyze and interpret information, data and facts
4. Analyze and develop solutions as well as make recommendations
5. Prepare report and sell recommendations
6. Install recommendations and follow up effectiveness

  b. Pitfalls to avoid
1. *Taking things for granted* – A statement of the situation does not necessarily imply that each of the elements is necessarily true; for example, a complaint may be invalid and biased so that all that can be taken for granted is that a complaint has been registered

2. *Considering only one side of a situation* – Wherever possible, indicate several alternatives and then point out the reasons you selected the best one
3. *Failing to indicate follow up* – Whenever your answer indicates action on your part, make certain that you will take proper follow-up action to see how successful your recommendations, procedures or actions turn out to be
4. *Taking too long in answering any single question* – Remember to time your answers properly

IX. AFTER THE TEST

Scoring procedures differ in detail among civil service jurisdictions although the general principles are the same. Whether the papers are hand-scored or graded by machine we have described, they are nearly always graded by number. That is, the person who marks the paper knows only the number – never the name – of the applicant. Not until all the papers have been graded will they be matched with names. If other tests, such as training and experience or oral interview ratings have been given, scores will be combined. Different parts of the examination usually have different weights. For example, the written test might count 60 percent of the final grade, and a rating of training and experience 40 percent. In many jurisdictions, veterans will have a certain number of points added to their grades.

After the final grade has been determined, the names are placed in grade order and an eligible list is established. There are various methods for resolving ties between those who get the same final grade – probably the most common is to place first the name of the person whose application was received first. Job offers are made from the eligible list in the order the names appear on it. You will be notified of your grade and your rank as soon as all these computations have been made. This will be done as rapidly as possible.

People who are found to meet the requirements in the announcement are called "eligibles." Their names are put on a list of eligible candidates. An eligible's chances of getting a job depend on how high he stands on this list and how fast agencies are filling jobs from the list.

When a job is to be filled from a list of eligibles, the agency asks for the names of people on the list of eligibles for that job. When the civil service commission receives this request, it sends to the agency the names of the three people highest on this list. Or, if the job to be filled has specialized requirements, the office sends the agency the names of the top three persons who meet these requirements from the general list.

The appointing officer makes a choice from among the three people whose names were sent to him. If the selected person accepts the appointment, the names of the others are put back on the list to be considered for future openings.

That is the rule in hiring from all kinds of eligible lists, whether they are for typist, carpenter, chemist, or something else. For every vacancy, the appointing officer has his choice of any one of the top three eligibles on the list. This explains why the person whose name is on top of the list sometimes does not get an appointment when some of the persons lower on the list do. If the appointing officer chooses the second or third eligible, the No. 1 eligible does not get a job at once, but stays on the list until he is appointed or the list is terminated.

X. HOW TO PASS THE INTERVIEW TEST

The examination for which you applied requires an oral interview test. You have already taken the written test and you are now being called for the interview test – the final part of the formal examination.

You may think that it is not possible to prepare for an interview test and that there are no procedures to follow during an interview. Our purpose is to point out some things you can do in advance that will help you and some good rules to follow and pitfalls to avoid while you are being interviewed.

What is an interview supposed to test?

The written examination is designed to test the technical knowledge and competence of the candidate; the oral is designed to evaluate intangible qualities, not readily measured otherwise, and to establish a list showing the relative fitness of each candidate – as measured against his competitors – for the position sought. Scoring is not on the basis of "right" and "wrong," but on a sliding scale of values ranging from "not passable" to "outstanding." As a matter of fact, it is possible to achieve a relatively low score without a single "incorrect" answer because of evident weakness in the qualities being measured.

Occasionally, an examination may consist entirely of an oral test – either an individual or a group oral. In such cases, information is sought concerning the technical knowledges and abilities of the candidate, since there has been no written examination for this purpose. More commonly, however, an oral test is used to supplement a written examination.

Who conducts interviews?

The composition of oral boards varies among different jurisdictions. In nearly all, a representative of the personnel department serves as chairman. One of the members of the board may be a representative of the department in which the candidate would work. In some cases, "outside experts" are used, and, frequently, a businessman or some other representative of the general public is asked to serve. Labor and management or other special groups may be represented. The aim is to secure the services of experts in the appropriate field.

However the board is composed, it is a good idea (and not at all improper or unethical) to ascertain in advance of the interview who the members are and what groups they represent. When you are introduced to them, you will have some idea of their backgrounds and interests, and at least you will not stutter and stammer over their names.

What should be done before the interview?

While knowledge about the board members is useful and takes some of the surprise element out of the interview, there is other preparation which is more substantive. It *is* possible to prepare for an oral interview – in several ways:

1) Keep a copy of your application and review it carefully before the interview

This may be the only document before the oral board, and the starting point of the interview. Know what education and experience you have listed there, and the sequence and dates of all of it. Sometimes the board will ask you to review the highlights of your experience for them; you should not have to hem and haw doing it.

2) Study the class specification and the examination announcement

Usually, the oral board has one or both of these to guide them. The qualities, characteristics or knowledges required by the position sought are stated in these documents. They offer valuable clues as to the nature of the oral interview. For example, if the job involves supervisory responsibilities, the announcement will usually indicate that knowledge of modern supervisory methods and the qualifications of the candidate as a supervisor will be tested. If so, you can expect such questions, frequently in the form of a hypothetical situation which you are expected to solve. NEVER go into an oral without knowledge of the duties and responsibilities of the job you seek.

3) Think through each qualification required

Try to visualize the kind of questions you would ask if you were a board member. How well could you answer them? Try especially to appraise your own knowledge and background in each area, *measured against the job sought*, and identify any areas in which you are weak. Be critical and realistic – do not flatter yourself.

4) Do some general reading in areas in which you feel you may be weak

For example, if the job involves supervision and your past experience has NOT, some general reading in supervisory methods and practices, particularly in the field of human relations, might be useful. Do NOT study agency procedures or detailed manuals. The oral board will be testing your understanding and capacity, not your memory.

5) Get a good night's sleep and watch your general health and mental attitude

You will want a clear head at the interview. Take care of a cold or any other minor ailment, and of course, no hangovers.

What should be done on the day of the interview?

Now comes the day of the interview itself. Give yourself plenty of time to get there. Plan to arrive somewhat ahead of the scheduled time, particularly if your appointment is in the fore part of the day. If a previous candidate fails to appear, the board might be ready for you a bit early. By early afternoon an oral board is almost invariably behind schedule if there are many candidates, and you may have to wait. Take along a book or magazine to read, or your application to review, but leave any extraneous material in the waiting room when you go in for your interview. In any event, relax and compose yourself.

The matter of dress is important. The board is forming impressions about you – from your experience, your manners, your attitude, and your appearance. Give your personal appearance careful attention. Dress your best, but not your flashiest. Choose conservative, appropriate clothing, and be sure it is immaculate. This is a business interview, and your appearance should indicate that you regard it as such. Besides, being well groomed and properly dressed will help boost your confidence.

Sooner or later, someone will call your name and escort you into the interview room. *This is it.* From here on you are on your own. It is too late for any more preparation. But remember, you asked for this opportunity to prove your fitness, and you are here because your request was granted.

What happens when you go in?

The usual sequence of events will be as follows: The clerk (who is often the board stenographer) will introduce you to the chairman of the oral board, who will introduce you to the other members of the board. Acknowledge the introductions before you sit down. Do not be surprised if you find a microphone facing you or a stenotypist sitting by. Oral interviews are usually recorded in the event of an appeal or other review.

Usually the chairman of the board will open the interview by reviewing the highlights of your education and work experience from your application – primarily for the benefit of the other members of the board, as well as to get the material into the record. Do not interrupt or comment unless there is an error or significant misinterpretation; if that is the case, do not hesitate. But do not quibble about insignificant matters. Also, he will usually ask you some question about your education, experience or your present job – partly to get you to start talking and to establish the interviewing "rapport." He may start the actual questioning, or turn it over to one of the other members. Frequently, each member undertakes the questioning on a particular area, one in which he is perhaps most competent, so you can expect each member to participate in the examination. Because time is limited, you may also expect some rather abrupt switches in the direction the questioning takes, so do not be upset by it. Normally, a board member will not pursue a single line of questioning unless he discovers a particular strength or weakness.

After each member has participated, the chairman will usually ask whether any member has any further questions, then will ask you if you have anything you wish to add. Unless you are expecting this question, it may floor you. Worse, it may start you off on an extended, extemporaneous speech. The board is not usually seeking more information. The question is principally to offer you a last opportunity to present further qualifications or to indicate that you have nothing to add. So, if you feel that a significant qualification or characteristic has been overlooked, it is proper to point it out in a sentence or so. Do not compliment the board on the thoroughness of their examination – they have been sketchy, and you know it. If you wish, merely say, "No thank you, I have nothing further to add." This is a point where you can "talk yourself out" of a good impression or fail to present an important bit of information. Remember, *you close the interview yourself*.

The chairman will then say, "That is all, Mr. _____, thank you." Do not be startled; the interview is over, and quicker than you think. Thank him, gather your belongings and take your leave. Save your sigh of relief for the other side of the door.

How to put your best foot forward

Throughout this entire process, you may feel that the board individually and collectively is trying to pierce your defenses, seek out your hidden weaknesses and embarrass and confuse you. Actually, this is not true. They are obliged to make an appraisal of your qualifications for the job you are seeking, and they want to see you in your best light. Remember, they must interview all candidates and a non-cooperative candidate may become a failure in spite of their best efforts to bring out his qualifications. Here are 15 suggestions that will help you:

1) Be natural – Keep your attitude confident, not cocky

If you are not confident that you can do the job, do not expect the board to be. Do not apologize for your weaknesses, try to bring out your strong points. The board is interested in a positive, not negative, presentation. Cockiness will antagonize any board member and make him wonder if you are covering up a weakness by a false show of strength.

2) Get comfortable, but don't lounge or sprawl

Sit erectly but not stiffly. A careless posture may lead the board to conclude that you are careless in other things, or at least that you are not impressed by the importance of the occasion. Either conclusion is natural, even if incorrect. Do not fuss with your clothing, a pencil or an ashtray. Your hands may occasionally be useful to emphasize a point; do not let them become a point of distraction.

3) Do not wisecrack or make small talk

This is a serious situation, and your attitude should show that you consider it as such. Further, the time of the board is limited – they do not want to waste it, and neither should you.

4) Do not exaggerate your experience or abilities

In the first place, from information in the application or other interviews and sources, the board may know more about you than you think. Secondly, you probably will not get away with it. An experienced board is rather adept at spotting such a situation, so do not take the chance.

5) If you know a board member, do not make a point of it, yet do not hide it

Certainly you are not fooling him, and probably not the other members of the board. Do not try to take advantage of your acquaintanceship – it will probably do you little good.

6) Do not dominate the interview

Let the board do that. They will give you the clues – do not assume that you have to do all the talking. Realize that the board has a number of questions to ask you, and do not try to take up all the interview time by showing off your extensive knowledge of the answer to the first one.

7) Be attentive

You only have 20 minutes or so, and you should keep your attention at its sharpest throughout. When a member is addressing a problem or question to you, give him your undivided attention. Address your reply principally to him, but do not exclude the other board members.

8) Do not interrupt

A board member may be stating a problem for you to analyze. He will ask you a question when the time comes. Let him state the problem, and wait for the question.

9) Make sure you understand the question

Do not try to answer until you are sure what the question is. If it is not clear, restate it in your own words or ask the board member to clarify it for you. However, do not haggle about minor elements.

10) Reply promptly but not hastily

A common entry on oral board rating sheets is "candidate responded readily," or "candidate hesitated in replies." Respond as promptly and quickly as you can, but do not jump to a hasty, ill-considered answer.

11) Do not be peremptory in your answers

A brief answer is proper – but do not fire your answer back. That is a losing game from your point of view. The board member can probably ask questions much faster than you can answer them.

12) Do not try to create the answer you think the board member wants

He is interested in what kind of mind you have and how it works – not in playing games. Furthermore, he can usually spot this practice and will actually grade you down on it.

13) Do not switch sides in your reply merely to agree with a board member

Frequently, a member will take a contrary position merely to draw you out and to see if you are willing and able to defend your point of view. Do not start a debate, yet do not surrender a good position. If a position is worth taking, it is worth defending.

14) Do not be afraid to admit an error in judgment if you are shown to be wrong

The board knows that you are forced to reply without any opportunity for careful consideration. Your answer may be demonstrably wrong. If so, admit it and get on with the interview.

15) Do not dwell at length on your present job

The opening question may relate to your present assignment. Answer the question but do not go into an extended discussion. You are being examined for a *new* job, not your present one. As a matter of fact, try to phrase ALL your answers in terms of the job for which you are being examined.

Basis of Rating

Probably you will forget most of these "do's" and "don'ts" when you walk into the oral interview room. Even remembering them all will not ensure you a passing grade. Perhaps you did not have the qualifications in the first place. But remembering them will help you to put your best foot forward, without treading on the toes of the board members.

Rumor and popular opinion to the contrary notwithstanding, an oral board wants you to make the best appearance possible. They know you are under pressure – but they also want to see how you respond to it as a guide to what your reaction would be under the pressures of the job you seek. They will be influenced by the degree of poise you display, the personal traits you show and the manner in which you respond.

ABOUT THIS BOOK

This book contains tests divided into Examination Sections. Go through each test, answering every question in the margin. We have also attached a sample answer sheet at the back of the book that can be removed and used. At the end of each test look at the answer key and check your answers. On the ones you got wrong, look at the right answer choice and learn. Do not fill in the answers first. Do not memorize the questions and answers, but understand the answer and principles involved. On your test, the questions will likely be different from the samples. Questions are changed and new ones added. If you understand these past questions you should have success with any changes that arise. Tests may consist of several types of questions. We have additional books on each subject should more study be advisable or necessary for you. Finally, the more you study, the better prepared you will be. This book is intended to be the last thing you study before you walk into the examination room. Prior study of relevant texts is also recommended. NLC publishes some of these in our Fundamental Series. Knowledge and good sense are important factors in passing your exam. Good luck also helps. So now study this Passbook, absorb the material contained within and take that knowledge into the examination. Then do your best to pass that exam.

EXAMINATION SECTION

EXAMINATION SECTION

TEST 1

DIRECTIONS: Each question or incomplete statement is followed by several suggested answers or completions. Select the one that BEST answers the question or completes the statement. *PRINT THE LETTER OF THE CORRECT ANSWER IN THE SPACE AT THE RIGHT.*

1. A supervisor may be required to help train a newly appointed clerk. Which of the following is LEAST important for a newly appointed clerk to know in order to perform his work efficiently?
    A. Acceptable ways of answering and recording telephone calls
    B. The number of files in the storage files unit
    C. The filing methods used by his unit
    D. Proper techniques for handling visitors

    1.____

2. In your agency you have the responsibility of processing clients who have appointments with agency representatives. On a particularly busy day, a client comes to your desk and insists that she must see the person handling her case although she has no appointment.
Under the circumstances, your FIRST action should be to
    A. show her the full appointment schedule
    B. give her an appointment for another day
    C. ask her to explain the urgency
    D. tell her to return later in the day

    2.____

3. Which of the following practices is BEST for a supervisor to use when assigning work to his staff?
    A. Give workers with seniority the most difficult jobs
    B. Assign all unimportant work to the slower workers
    C. Permit each employee to pick the job he prefers
    D. Make assignments based on the workers' abilities

    3.____

4. In which of the following instances is a supervisor MOST justified in giving commands to people under his supervision? When
    A. they delay in following instructions which have been given to them clearly
    B. they become relaxed and slow about work, and he wants to speed up their production
    C. he must direct them in an emergency situation
    D. he is instructing them on jobs that are unfamiliar to them

    4.____

5. Which of the following supervisory actions or attitudes is MOST likely to result in getting subordinates to try to do as much work as possible for a supervisor? He
    A. shows that his most important interest is in schedules and production goals
    B. consistently pressures his staff to get the work out

    5.____

1

C. never fails to let them know he is in charge
D. considers their abilities and needs while requiring that production goals be met

6. Assume that a supervisor has been explaining certain regulations to a new clerk under his supervision.
   The MOST efficient way for the supervisor to make sure that the clerk has understood the explanation is to
   A. give him written materials on the regulations
   B. ask him if he has any further questions about the regulations
   C. ask him specific questions based on what has just been explained to him
   D. watch the way he handles a situation involving these regulations

7. One of your unit clerks has been assigned to work for a Mr. Jones in another office for several days. At the end of the first day, Mr. Jones, saying the clerk was not satisfactory, asks that she not be assigned to him again. This clerk is one of your most dependable workers, and no previous complaints about her work have come to you from any other outside assignments.
   To get to the root of this situation, your FIRST action should be to
   A. ask Mr. Jones to explain in what way her work was unsatisfactory
   B. ask the clerk what she did that Mr. Jones considered unsatisfactory
   C. check with supervisors for whom she previously worked to see if your own rating of her is in error
   D. tell Mr. Jones to pick the clerk he would prefer to have work for him the next time

8. A senior typist, still on probation, is instructed to type, as quickly as possible, one section of a draft of a long, complex report. Her part must be typed and readable before another part of the report can be written. Asked when she can have the report ready, she gives her supervisor an estimate of a day longer than she knows it will actually take. She then finishes the job a day sooner than the date given her supervisor.
   The judgment shown by the senior typist in giving an overestimate of time in a situation like this is, in general,
   A. *good*, because it prevents the supervisor from thinking she works slowly
   B. *good*, because it keeps unrealistic supervisors from expecting too much
   C. *bad*, because she should have used the time left to further check and proofread her work
   D. *bad*, because schedules and plans for other parts of the project may have been based on her false estimate

9. Suppose a new clerk, still on probation, is placed under your supervision and refuses to do a job you ask him to do.
   What is the FIRST thing you should do?
   A. Explain that you are the supervisor and he must follow your instructions
   B. Tell him he may be suspended if he refuses
   C. Ask someone else to do the job and rate him accordingly
   D. Ask for his reason for objecting to the request

10. As a supervisor of a small group of people, you have blamed worker A for something that you later find out was really done by worker B.
The BEST thing for you to do now would be to
   A. say nothing to worker A but criticize worker B for his mistake while worker A is near so that A will realize that you know who made the mistake
   B. speak to each worker separately, apologize to worker A for your mistake, and discuss worker B's mistake with him
   C. bring both workers together, apologize to worker A for your mistake, and discuss worker B's mistake with him
   D. say nothing now but be careful about mixing up worker A with worker B in the future

11. You have just learned one of your staff is grumbling that she thinks you are not pleased with her work. As far as you're concerned, this isn't true at all. In fact, you've paid no particular attention to this worker lately because you've been very busy. You have just finished preparing an important report and *breaking in* a new clerk.
Under the circumstances, the BEST thing to do is
   A. ignore her; after all, it's just a figment of her imagination
   B. discuss the matter with her now to try to find out and eliminate the cause of this problem
   C. tell her not to worry about it; you haven't had time to think about her work
   D. make a note to meet with her at a later date in order to straighten out the situation

12. A most important job of a supervisor is to positively motivate employees to increase their work production.
Which of the following LEAST indicates that a group of workers has been positively motivated?
   A. Their work output becomes constant and stable.
   B. Their cooperation at work becomes greater.
   C. They begin to show pride in the product of their work.
   D. They show increased interest in their work

13. Which of the following traits would be LEAST important in considering a person for a merit increase?
   A. Punctuality
   B. Using initiative successfully
   C. High rate of production
   D. Resourcefulness

14. Of the following, the action LEAST likely to gain a supervisor the cooperation of his staff is for him to
   A. give each person consideration as an individual
   B. be as objective as possible when evaluating work performance
   C. rotate the least popular assignments
   D. expect subordinates to be equally competent

15. It has been said that, for the supervisor, nothing can beat the *face-to-face* communication of talking to one subordinate at a time.
    This method is, however, LEAST appropriate to use when
    A. supervisor is explaining a change in general office procedure
    B. subject is of personal importance
    C. supervisor is conducting a yearly performance evaluation of all employees
    D. supervisor must talk to some of his employees concerning their poor attendance and punctuality

16. While you are on the telephone answering a question about your agency, a visitor comes to your desk and starts to ask you a question. There is no emergency or urgency in either situation, that of the phone call or that of answering the visitor's question.
    In this case, you should
    A. continue to answer the person on the telephone until you are finished and then tell the visitor you are sorry to have kept him waiting
    B. excuse yourself to the person on the telephone and tell the visitor that you will be with him as soon as you have finished on the phone
    C. explain to the person on the telephone that you have a visitor and must shorten the conversation
    D. continue to answer the person on the phone while looking up occasionally at the visitor to let him know that you know he is waiting

17. While speaking on the telephone to someone who called, you are disconnected.
    The FIRST thing you should do is
    A. hang up but try to keep your line free to receive the call back
    B. immediately get the dial tone and continually dial the person who called you until you reach him
    C. signal the switchboard operator and ask her to re-establish the connection
    D. dial O for Operator and explain that you were disconnected

18. The type of speech used by an office worker in telephone conversations greatly affects the communicator.
    Of the following, the BEST way to express your ideas when telephoning is with a vocabulary that consists mainly of _____ words.
    A. formal, intellectual sounding   B. often used colloquial
    C. technical, emphatic   D. simple, descriptive

19. Suppose a clerk under your supervision has taken a personal phone call and is at the same time needed to answer a question regarding an assignment being handled by another member of your office. He appears confused as to what he should do. How should you instruct him later as to how to handle a similar situation?
    You should tell him to
    A. tell the caller to hold on while he answers the question
    B. tell the caller to call back a little later

C. return the call during an assigned break
D. finish the conversation quickly and answer the question

20. You are asked to place a telephone call by your supervisor. When you place the call, you receive what appears to be a wrong number.
Of the following, you should FIRST
A. check the number with your supervisor to see if the number he gave you is correct
B. ask the person on the other end what his number is and who he is
C. check with the person on the other end to see if the number you dialed is the number you received
D. apologize to the person on the other end for disturbing him and hang up

20.____

Questions 21-30.

DIRECTIONS: WORD MEANING
Each of Questions 21 through 30 contains a word in capitals followed by four suggested meanings of the word. For each question, choose the BEST meaning and write the letter of the best meaning in the space at the right.

21. ACCURATE
    A. correct   B. useful   C. afraid   D. careless

21.____

22. ALTER
    A. copy   B. change   C. repeat   D. agree

22.____

23. DOCUMENT
    A. outline   B. agreement   C. blueprint   D. record

23.____

24. INDICATE
    A. listen   B. show   C. guess   D. try

24.____

25. INVENTORY
    A. custom   B. discovery   C. warning   D. list

25.____

26. ISSUE
    A. annoy   B. use up   C. give out   D. gain

26.____

27. NOTIFY
    A. inform   B. promise   C. approve   D. strength

27.____

28. ROUTINE
    A. path   B. mistake   C. habit   D. journey

28.____

29. TERMINATE
    A. rest   B. start   C. deny   D. end

29.____

30. TRANSMIT
    A. put in   B. send   C. stop   D. go across

30.____

Questions 31-35.

DIRECTIONS: READING COMPREHENSION
Questions 31 through 35 test how well you understand what you read. It will be necessary for you to read carefully because your answers to these questions should be based SOLELY on the information given in the following paragraphs.

The recipient gains an impression of a typewritten letter before he begins to read the message. Factors which provide for a good first impression include margins and spacing that are visually pleasing, formal parts of the letter which are correctly placed according to the style of the letter, copy which is free of obvious erasures and over-strikes, and transcript that is even and clear. The problem for the typist is that of how to produce that first, positive impression of her work.

There are several general rules which a typist can follow when she wishes to prepare a properly spaced letter on a sheet of letterhead. Ordinarily, the width of a letter should not be less than four inches nor more than six inches. The side margins should also have a desirable relation to the bottom margin and the space between the letterhead and the body of the letter. Usually the most appealing arrangement is when the side margins are even and the bottom margin is slightly wider than the side margins. In some offices, however, standard line length is used for all business letters, and the secretary then varies the spacing between the date line and the inside address according to the length of the letter.

31. The BEST title for the above paragraphs would be   31._____
    A. Writing Office Letters
    B. Making Good First Impressions
    C. Judging Well-Typed Letters
    D. Good Placing and Spacing for Office Letters

32. According to the above paragraphs, which of the following might be considered   32._____
    the way in which people very quickly judge the quality of work which has been
    typed?
    By
    A. measuring the margins to see if they are correct
    B. looking at the spacing and cleanliness of the typescript
    C. scanning the body of the letter for meaning
    D. reading the date line and address for errors

33. What, according to the above paragraphs, would be definitely UNDESIRABLE   33._____
    as the average line length of a typed letter?
       A. 4"   B. 5"   C. 6"   D. 7"

34. According to the above paragraphs, when the line length is kept standard,   34._____
    the secretary
    A. does not have to vary the spacing at all since this also is standard
    B. adjusts the spacing between the date line and inside address for different
       lengths of letters
    C. uses the longest line as a guideline for spacing between the date line and
       inside address
    D. varies the number of spaces between the lines

35. According to the above paragraphs, side margins are MOST pleasing when they   35._____
    A. are even and somewhat smaller than the bottom margin
    B. are slightly wider than the bottom margin
    C. vary with the length of the letter
    D. are figured independently from the letterhead and the body of the letter

Questions 36-40.

DIRECTIONS: CODING

        Name of Applicant   H A N G S B R U K E
        Test Code   c o m p l e x i t y
        File Number   0 1 2 3 4 5 6 7 8 9

Assume that each of the above capital letters is the first letter of the name of an applicant, that the small letter directly beneath each capital letter is the test code for the applicant, and that the number directly beneath each code letter is the file number for the applicant.

In each of the following Questions 36 through 40, the test code letters and the file numbers in Columns 2 and 3 should correspond to the capital letters in Column 1. For each question, look at each column carefully and mark your answer as follows:
    If there is an error only in Column 2, mark your answer A.
    If there is an error only in Column 3, mark your answer B.
    If there is an error in both Columns 2 and 3, mark your answer C.
    If both Columns 2 and 3 are correct, mark your answer D.

The following sample question is given to help you understand the procedure.

SAMPLE QUESTION

Column 1	Column 2	Column 3
AKEHN	otyci	18902

In Column 2, the final test code letter *i* should be *m*. Column 3 is correctly coded in Column 1. Since there is an error only in Column 2, the answer is A.

#	Column 1	Column 2	Column 3	
36.	NEKKU	mytti	29987	36._____
37.	KRAEB	txlye	86095	37._____
38.	ENAUK	ymoit	92178	38._____
39.	REANA	xeomo	69121	39._____
40.	EKHSE	ytcxy	97049	

Questions 41-50.

DIRECTIONS: ARITHMETICAL REASONING
Solve the following problems.

41. If a secretary answered 28 phone calls and typed the addresses for 112 credit statements in one morning, what is the RATIO of phone calls answered to credit statements typed for that period of time?
    A. 1:4 B. 1:7 C. 2:3 D. 3:5

42. According to a suggested filing system, no more than 10 folders should be filed behind any one file guide, and from 15 to 25 file guides should be used in each file drawer for easy finding and filing.
    The MAXIMUM number of folders that a five-drawer file cabinet can hold to allow easy finding and filing is
    A. 550 B. 750 C. 1,100 D. 1,250

43. An employee had a starting salary of $32,902. He received a salary increase at the end of each year, and at the end of the seventh year, his salary was $36,738.
    What was his AVERAGE annual increase in salary over these seven years?
    A. $510 B. $538 C. $548 D. $572

44. The 55 typists and 28 senior clerks in a certain agency were paid a total of $1,943,200 in salaries for the year.
    If the average annual salary of a typist was $22,400, the average annual salary of a senior clerk was
    A. $25,400 B. $26,600 C. $26,800 D. $27,000

45. A typist has been given a three-page report to type. She has finished typing the first two pages. The first page has 283 words, and the second page has 366 words.
    If the total report consists of 954 words, how many words will she have to type on the third page of the report?
    A. 202 B. 287 C. 305 D. 313

46. In one day, Clerk A processed 30% more forms than Clerk B, and Clerk C processed 11/4 as many forms as Clerk A.
    If Clerk B processed 40 forms, how many MORE forms were processed by Clerk C?
    A. 12 B. 13 C. 21 D. 25

47. A clerk who earns a gross salary of $452 every week has the following deductions taken from her paycheck: 17½% for City, State, Federal taxes, and for Social Security, $1.20 for health insurance, and $6.10 for union dues.
    The amount of her take-home pay is
    A. $286.40 B. $312.40 C. $331.60 D. $365.60

48. In 2022 an agency spent $400 to buy pencils at a cost of $1 a dozen. 48._____
If the agency used ¾ of these pencils in 2022 and used the same number of
pencils in 2023, how many MORE pencils did it have to buy to have enough
pencils for all of 2023?
   A. 1,200   B. 2,400   C. 3,600   D. 4,800

49. A clerk who worked in Agency X earned the following salaries: $30,070 the 49._____
first year, $30,500 the second year, and $30,960 the third year. Another clerk
who worked in Agency Y for three years earned $30,550 a year for two years
and $30,724 the third year.
The DIFFERENCE between the average salaries received by both clerks over
a three-year period is
   A. $98   B. $102   C. $174   D. $282

50. An employee who works over 40 hours in any week receives overtime payment 50._____
for the extra hours at time and one-half (1½ times) his hourly rate of pay. An
employee who earns $15.60 an hour works a total of 45 hours during a certain
week.
His TOTAL pay for that week would be
   A. $624.00   B. $702.00   C. $741.00   D. $824.00

KEY (CORRECT ANSWERS)

1.	B	11.	B	21.	A	31.	D	41.	A
2.	C	12.	A	22.	B	32.	B	42.	D
3.	D	13.	A	23.	D	33.	D	43.	C
4.	C	14.	D	24.	B	34.	B	44.	A
5.	D	15.	A	25.	D	35.	A	45.	C
6.	C	16.	B	26.	C	36.	B	46.	D
7.	A	17.	A	27.	A	37.	C	47.	D
8.	D	18.	D	28.	C	38.	D	48.	B
9.	D	19.	C	29.	D	39.	A	49.	A
10.	B	20.	C	30.	B	40.	C	50.	C

TEST 2

DIRECTIONS: Each question or incomplete statement is followed by several suggested answers or completions. Select the one that BEST answers the question or completes the statement. *PRINT THE LETTER OF THE CORRECT ANSWER IN THE SPACE AT THE RIGHT.*

1. To tell a newly employed clerk to fill a top drawer of a four-drawer cabinet with heavy folders which will be often used and to keep lower drawers only partly filled is
    A. *good*, because a tall person would have to bend unnecessarily if he had to use a lower drawer
    B. *bad*, because the file cabinet may tip over when the top drawer is opened
    C. *good*, because it is the most easily reachable drawer for the average person
    D. *bad*, because a person bending down at another drawer may accidentally bang his head on the bottom of the drawer when he straightens up

2. If you have requisitioned a ream of paper in order to duplicate a single page office announcement, how many announcements can be printed from the one package of paper?
    A. 200   B. 500   C. 700   D. 1,000

3. In the operations of a government agency, a voucher is ORDINARILY used to
    A. refer someone to the agency for a position or assignment
    B. certify that an agency's records of financial transactions are accurate
    C. order payment from agency funds of a stated amount to an individual
    D. enter a statement of official opinion in the records of the agency

4. Of the following types of cards used in filing systems, the one which is generally MOST helpful in locating records which might be filed under more than one subject is the _____ card.
    A. cut
    B. tickler
    C. cross-reference
    D. visible index

5. The type of filing system in which one does NOT need to refer to a card index in order to find the folder is called
    A. alphabetic   B. geographic   C. subject   D. locational

6. Of the following, records management is LEAST concerned with
    A. the development of the best method for retrieving important information
    B. deciding what records should be kept
    C. deciding the number of appointments a client will need
    D. determining the types of folders to be used

7. If records are continually removed from a set of files without *charging* them to the borrower, the filing system will soon become ineffective.
   Of the following terms, the one which is NOT applied to a form used in a charge-out system is a
   A. requisition card
   B. out-folder
   C. record retrieval form
   D. substitution card

7.____

8. A new clerk has been told to put 500 cards in alphabetical order. Another clerk suggests that she divide the cards into four groups such as A to F, G to L, M to R, and S to Z, and then alphabetize these four smaller groups.
   The suggested method is
   A. *poor*, because the clerk will have to handle the sheets more than once and will waste time
   B. *good*, because it saves time, is more accurate, and is less tiring
   C. *good*, because she will not have to concentrate on it so much when it is in smaller groups
   D. *bad*, because this method is much more tiring than straight alphabetizing

8.____

9. The term that describes the equipment attached to an office computer is
   A. interface   B. network   C. hardware   D. software

9.____

10. Suppose a clerk has been given pads of pre-printed forms to use when taking phone messages for others in her office. The clerk is then observed using scraps of paper and not the forms for writing her messages.
    It should be explained that the BEST reason for using the forms is that
    A. they act as a checklist to make sure that the important information is taken
    B. she is expected to do her work in the same way as others in the office
    C. they make sure that unassigned paper is not wasted on phone messages
    D. learning to use these forms will help train her to use more difficult forms

10.____

11. Of the following, the one which is spelled INCORRECTLY is
    A. alphabetization
    B. reccommendation
    C. redaction
    D. synergy

11.____

12. Of the following, the MAIN reason a stock clerk keeps a perpetual inventory of supplies in the storeroom is that such an inventory will
    A. eliminate the need for a physical inventory
    B. provide a continuous record of supplies on hand
    C. indicate whether a shipment of supplies is satisfactory
    D. dictate the terms of the purchase order

12.____

13. As a supervisor, you may be required to handle different types of correspondence.
    Of the following types of letters, it would be MOST important to promptly seal which kind of letters?

13.____

A. One marked *confidential*
B. Those containing enclosures
C. Any letter to be sent airmail
D. Those in which carbons will be sent along with the original

14. While opening incoming mail, you notice that one letter indicates that an enclosure was to be included but, even after careful inspection,, you are not able to find the information to which this refers.
Of the following, the thing that you should do FIRST is
    A. replace the letter in its envelope and return it to the sender
    B. file the letter until the sender's office mails the missing information
    C. type out a letter to the sender informing them of their error
    D. make a notation in the margin of the letter that the enclosure was omitted

14.____

15. You have been given a checklist and assigned the responsibility of inspecting certain equipment in the various offices of your agency.
Which of the following is the GREATEST advantage of the checklist?
    A. It indicates which equipment is in greatest demand.
    B. Each piece of equipment on the checklist will be checked only once.
    C. It helps to insure that the equipment listed will not be overlooked.
    D. The equipment listed suggests other equipment you should look for.

15.____

16. Your supervisor has asked you to locate a telephone number for an attorney named Jones, whose office is located at 311 Broadway and whose name is not already listed in your files.
The BEST method for finding the number would be for you to
    A. call the information operator and have her get it for you
    B. look in the alphabetical directory (white pages) under the name Jones at 311 Broadway
    C. refer to the heading Attorney in the yellow pages for the name Jones at 311 Broadway
    D. ask your supervisor who referred her to Mr. Jones, then call that person for the number

16.____

17. An example of material that should NOT be sent by first class mail is a
    A. carbon copy of a letter   B. postcard
    C. business reply card   D. large catalogue

17.____

18. Which of the following BEST describes *office work simplification*?
    A. An attempt to increase the rate of production by speeding up the movements of employees
    B. Eliminating wasteful steps in order to increase efficiency
    C. Making jobs as easy as possible for employees so they will not be overworked
    D. Eliminating all difficult tasks from an office and leaving only simple ones

18.____

19. The duties of a supervisor who is assigned the job of timekeeper may include all of the following EXCEPT   19.____
    A. computing and recording regular hours worked each day in accordance with the normal work schedule
    B. approving requests for vacation leave, sick leave, and annual leave
    C. computing and recording overtime hours worked beyond the normal schedule
    D. determining the total regular hours and total extra hours worked during the week

20. Suppose a clerk under your supervision accidentally opens a personal letter while handling office mail.   20.____
    Under such circumstances, you should tell the clerk to put the letter back in the envelope and
    A. take the letter to the person to whom it belongs and make sure he understands that the clerk did not read it
    B. try to seal the envelope so it won't appear to have been opened
    C. write on the envelope *Sorry, opened by mistake*, and put his initials on it
    D. write on the envelope *Sorry, opened by mistake*, but not put his initials on it

Questions 21-25.

DIRECTIONS: SPELLING
Each Question 21 through 25 consists of three words. In each question, one of the words may be spelled incorrectly or all three may be spelled correctly. For each question, if one of the words is spelled incorrectly, write the letter of the incorrect word in the space at the right. If all three words are spelled correctly, write the letter D in the space at the right.

SAMPLE I: (A) guide   (B) departmint   (C) stranger
SAMPLE II: (A) comply   (B) valuable   (C) window

In Sample Question I, *departmint* is incorrect. It should be spelled *department*. Therefore, B is the answer to Sample Question 1.
In Sample Question II, all three words are spelled correctly. Therefore D is the answer to Sample Question II.

21.	A.	argument	B.	reciept	C.	complain	21.____
22.	A.	sufficient	B.	postpone	C.	visible	22.____
23.	A.	expirience	B.	dissatisfy	C.	alternate	23.____
24.	A.	occurred	B.	noticable	C.	appendix	24.____
25.	A.	anxious	B.	guarantee	C.	calender	25.____

Questions 26-30.

DIRECTIONS: ENGLISH USAGE
Each Question 26 through 30 contains a sentence. Read each sentence carefully to decide whether it is correct. Then, in the space at the right, mark your answer:
A. if the sentence is incorrect because of bad grammar or sentence structure
B. of the sentence is incorrect because of bad punctuation
C. if the sentence is incorrect because of bad capitalization
D. if the sentence is correct

Each incorrect sentence has only one type of error. Consider a sentence correct if it has no errors, although there may be other correct ways of saying the same thing.

SAMPLE QUESTION I: One of our clerks were promoted yesterday.
The subject of this sentence is *one*, so the verb should be *was promoted* instead of *were promoted*. Since the sentence is incorrect because of bad grammar, the answer to Sample Question I is A.

SAMPLE QUESTION II: Between you and me, I would prefer not going there.
Since this sentence is correct, the answer to Sample Question II is D.

26. The National alliance of Businessmen is trying to persuade private businesses to hire youth in the summertime.   26.____

27. The supervisor who is on vacation, is in charge of processing vouchers.   27.____

28. The activity of the committee at its conferences is always stimulating.   28.____

29. After checking the addresses again, the letters went to the mailroom.   29.____

30. The director, as well as the employees, are interested in sharing the dividends.   30.____

Questions 31-40.

DIRECTIONS: FILING
Each Question 31 through 40 contains four names. For each question, choose the name that should be FIRST if the four names are to be arranged in alphabetical order in accordance with the Rules for Alphabetical Filing given below. Read these rules carefully. Then, for each question, indicate in the correspondingly numbered space at the right the letter before the name that should be FIRST in alphabetical order.

RULES FOR ALPHABETICAL FILING

Names of People

1. The names of people are filed in strict alphabetical order, first according to the last name, then according to first name or initial, and finally according to middle name or initial. For example: George Allen comes before Edward Bell, and Leonard P. Reston comes before Lucille B. Reston.

2. When last names are the same, for example A. Green and Agnes Green, the one with the initial comes before the one with the name written out when the first initials are identical.

3. When first and last names are alike and the middle initial is given, for example John David Doe and John Devoe Doe, the names should be filed in the alphabetical order of the middle names.

4. When first and last names are the same, a name without a middle initial comes before one with a middle name or initial. For example, John Doe comes before both John A. Doe and John Alan Doe.

5. When first and last names are the same, a name with a middle initial comes before one with a middle name beginning with the same initial. For example: Jack R. Herts comes before Jack Richard Hertz.

6. Prefixes such as De, O', Mac, Mc, and Van are filed as written and are treated as part of the names to which they are connected. For example: Robert O'Dea is filed before David Olsen.

7. Abbreviated names are treated as if they were spelled out. For example: Chas. is filed as Charles and Thos. is filed as Thomas.

8. Titles and designations such as Dr., Mr., and Prof. are disregarded in filing.

Names of Organizations

1. The names of business organizations are filed according to the order in which each word in the name appears. When an organization name bears the name of a person, it is filed according to the rules for filing names of people as given above. For example, William Smith Service Co. comes before Television Distributors, Inc.

2. Where bureau, board, office or department appears as the first part of the title of a governmental agency, that agency should be filed under the word in the title expressing the chief function of the agency. For example: Bureau of the Budget would be filed as if written Budget, (Bureau of the). The Department of Personnel would be filed as if written Personnel (Department of).

3. When the following words are part of an organization, they are disregarded: the, of, and.

4. When there are numbers in a name, they are treated as if they were spelled out. For example: 10th Street Bootery is filed as Tenth Street Bootery.

SAMPLE QUESTION: A. Jane Earl   (2)
                  B. James A. Earle   (4)
                  C. James Earl   (1)
                  D. J. Earle   (3)

The numbers in parentheses show the proper alphabetical order in which these names should be filed. Since the name that should be filed FIRST is James Earl, the answer to the sample question is C.

31. A. Majorca Leather Goods   B. Robert Majorca and Sons   31._____
    C. Maintenance Management Corp.   D. Majestic Carpet Mills

32. A. Municipal Telephone Service   B. Municipal Reference Library   32._____
    C. Municipal Credit Union   D. Municipal Broadcasting System

33. A. Robert B. Pierce   B. R. Bruce Pierce   33._____
    C. Ronald Pierce   D. Robert Bruce Pierce

34. A. Four Seasons Sports Club   B. 14 Street Shopping Center   34._____
    C. Forty Thieves Restaurant   D. 42nd St. Theaters

35. A. Franco Franceschini   B. Amos Franchini   35._____
    C. Sandra Franceschia   D. Lilie Franchinesca

36. A. Chas. A. Levine   B. Kurt Levene   36._____
    C. Charles Levine   D. Kurt E. Levene

37. A. Prof. Geo. Kinkaid   B. Mr. Alan Kinkaid   37._____
    C. Dr. Albert A. Kinkade   D. Kincade Liquors Inc.

38. A. Department of Public Events   B. Office of the Public Administrator 38._____
    C. Queensborough Public Library   D. Department of Public Health

39. A. Martin Luther King, Jr. Towers   B. Metro North Plaza   39._____
    C. Manhattanville Houses   D. Marble Hill Houses

40. A. Dr. Arthur Davids   B. The David Check Cashing Service 40._____
    C. A.C. Davidsen   D. Milton Davidoff

Questions 41-45.

DIRECTIONS: READING COMPREHENSION
Questions 41 through 45 test how well you understand what you read. It will be necessary for you to read carefully because your answers to these questions should be based SOLELY on the information given in the following paragraph.

8 (#2)

Work standards presuppose an ability to measure work. Measurement in office management is needed for several reasons. First, it is necessary to evaluate the overall efficiency of the office itself. It is then essential to measure the efficiency of each particular section or unit and that of the individual worker. To plan and control the work of sections and units, one must have measurement. A program of measurement goes hand in hand with a program of standards. One can have measurement without standards, but one cannot have work standards without measurement. Providing data on amount of work done and time expended, measurement does not deal with the amount of energy expended by an individual although in many cases such energy may be in direct proportion to work output. Usually from two-thirds to three fourths of all work can be measured. However, less than two-thirds of all work is actually measured because measurement difficulties are encountered when office work is non-repetitive and irregular, or when it is primarily mental rather than manual. These obstacles are often used as excuses for non-measurement far more frequently than is justified.

41. According to the paragraph, an office manager cannot set work standards unless he can
    A. plan the amount of work to be done
    B. control the amount of work that is done
    C. estimate accurately the quantity of work done
    D. delegate the amount of work to be done to efficient workers

42. According to the paragraph, the type of office work that would be MOST difficult to measure would be
    A. checking warrants for accuracy of information
    B. recording payroll changes
    C. processing applications
    D. making up a new system of giving out supplies

43. According to the paragraph, the actual amount of work that is measured is _____ of all work.
    A. less than two-thirds
    B. two-thirds to three-fourths
    C. less than three-sixths
    D. more than three-fourths

44. Which of the following would be MOST difficult to determine by using measurement techniques?
    A. The amount of work that is accomplished during a certain period of time
    B. The amount of work that should be planned for a period of time
    C. How much time is needed to do a certain task
    D. The amount of incentive a person must have to do his job

45. The one of the following which is the MOST suitable title for the paragraph is:
    A. How Measurement of Office Efficiency Depends on Work Standards
    B. Using Measurement for Office Management and Efficiency
    C. Work Standards and the Efficiency of the Office Worker
    D. Managing the Office Using Measured Work Standards

Questions 46-50.

DIRECTIONS: INTERPRETING STATISTICAL DATA
Questions 46 through 50 are to be answered using the information given in the following table.

AGE COMPOSITION IN THE LABOR FORCE IN CITY A
(2010-2020)

	Age Group	2010	2015	2020
Men	14-24	8,430	10,900	14,340
	25-44	22,200	22,350	26,065
	45+	17,550	19,800	21,970
Women	14-24	4,450	6,915	7,680
	25-44	9,080	10,010	11,550
	45+	7,325	9,470	13,180

46. The GREATEST increase in the number of people in the labor force between 2010 and 2015 occurred among
    A. men between the ages of 14 and 24
    B. men age 45 and over
    C. women between the ages of 14 and 24
    D. women age 45 and over

47. If the total number of women of all ages in the labor force increases from 2020 to 2025 by the same number as it did from 2015 to 2020, the TOTAL number of women of all ages in the labor force in 2025 will be
    A. 27,425   B. 29,675   C. 37,525   D. 38,425

48. The total increase in number of women in the labor force from 2010 to 2015 differs from the total increase of men in the same years by being _____ than that of men.
    A. 770 less   B. 670 more   C. 770 more   D. 1,670 more

49. In the year 2010, the proportion of married women in each group was as follows: 1/5 of the women in the 14-24 age group, 1/4 of those in the 25-44 age group, and 2/5 of those 45 and over.
    How many married women were in the labor force in 2010?
    A. 4,625   B. 5,990   C. 6,090   D. 7,910

50. The 14-24 age group of men in the labor force from 2010 to 2020 increased by APPROXIMATELY
    A. 40%   B. 65%   C. 70%   D. 75%

KEY (CORRECT ANSWERS)

1. B	11. B	21. B	31. C	41. C
2. B	12. B	22. D	32. D	42. D
3. C	13. A	23. A	33. B	43. A
4. C	14. D	24. B	34. D	44. D
5. A	15. C	25. C	35. C	45. B
6. C	16. C	26. C	36. B	46. A
7. C	17. D	27. B	37. D	47. D
8. B	18. B	28. D	38. B	48. B
9. C	19. B	29. A	39. A	49. C
10. A	20. C	30. A	40. B	50. C

EXAMINATION SECTION
TEST 1

DIRECTIONS: Each question or incomplete statement is followed by several suggested answers or completions. Select the one that BEST answers the question or completes the statement. *PRINT THE LETTER OF THE CORRECT ANSWER IN THE SPACE AT THE RIGHT.*

1. When you select someone to serve as supervisor of your unit during your absence on vacation and at other times, it would generally be BEST to choose the employee who is

   A. able to move the work along smoothly without friction
   B. on staff longest
   C. liked best by the rest of the staff
   D. able to perform the work of each employee to be supervised

2. Successful supervision of handicapped persons employed in a department depends MOST on providing them with a work place and work climate

   A. which is safe and accident-free
   B. that requires close and direct supervision by others
   C. that requires the performance of routine, repetitive tasks under a minimum of pressure
   D. where they will be accepted by the other employees

3. Studies have indicated that when employees feel that their work is aimless and unchallenging, the allocation or payment of more money for this type of work is LIKELY to

   A. contribute little to increased production
   B. bring more status to this work
   C. increase employees' feelings of security
   D. give employees greater motivation

4. An employee's performance has fallen below established minimum standards of quantity and quality.
   The threat of monetary or other disciplinary action as a device for improving this employee's performance would PROBABLY be acceptable and most effective

   A. only if applied as soon as the performance fell below standard
   B. only after more constructive techniques have failed
   C. at any time provided the employee understands that the punishment will be carried out
   D. at no time

5. A supervisor must, on short notice, ask his staff to work overtime.
   Of the following, a technique that is MOST likely to win their willing cooperation would be to

   A. explain that occasional overtime is part of the job requirement
   B. explain that they will be doing him a personal favor which he will appreciate very much
   C. explain why the overtime is necessary
   D. promise them that they can take the extra time off in the near future

6. On checking a completed work assignment of an employee, the supervisor finds that the work was not done correctly because the employee had not understood his instructions. Of the following, the BEST way to prevent repetition of this situation next time is for the supervisor to

   A. ask the employee whether he fully understood the instructions and tell him to ask questions in the future whenever anything is unclear
   B. ask the employee to repeat the instructions given and test his understanding with several key questions
   C. give the instructions a second time, emphasizing the more complicated aspects of the job
   D. give work instructions in writing

7. If, as a supervisor, you find yourself pressured for time to handle all of your job responsibilities, the one of the following tasks which it would be MOST appropriate for you to delegate to a subordinate is

   A. attending a staff conference of unit supervisors to discuss the implementation of a new departmental policy
   B. making staff work assignments
   C. interviewing a new employee
   D. checking work of certain employees for accuracy

8. Suppose you are unavoidably late for work one morning. When you arrive at 10 o'clock, you find there are several matters demanding your attention.
   Which one of the following matters should you handle LAST?

   A. A visitor who had a 9:30 appointment with you has been waiting to see you since 9 o'clock
   B. An employee on an assignment which should have been completed that morning is absent, and the work will have to be reassigned
   C. Several letters which you dictated at the end of the previous day have been typed and are on your desk for signature and mailing
   D. Your superior called asking you to get certain information for him when you come in and to call him back

9. Suppose that you have assigned a typist to type a report containing considerable statistical and tabular material and have given her specific instructions as to how this material is to be laid out on each page. When she returns the completed report, you find that it was not prepared according to your instructions, but you may possibly be able to use it the way it was typed. When you question her, she states that she thought her layout was better, but you were unavailable for consultation when she began the work.
   Of the following, the BEST action for you to take is to

   A. criticize her for not doing the work according to your instructions
   B. have her retype the report
   C. praise her for her work but tell her she could have waited until she could consult you
   D. praise her for using initiative

10. Of the following, the MOST effective way for a supervisor to correct poor working habits of an employee which result in low and poor quality output is to give the employee

A. additional training
B. less demanding assignments until his work improves
C. continuous supervision
D. more severe criticism

11. Of the following, the BEST way for a supervisor to teach an employee how to do a new and somewhat complicated job is to

    A. assign him to observe another employee who is already skilled in this work and instruct him to consult this employee if he has any questions
    B. explain to him how to do it, then demonstrate how it is done, then observe and correct the employee as he does it, then follow up
    C. give him a written, detailed, step-by-step explanation of how to do the job and instruct him to ask questions if anything is unclear when he does the work
    D. teach him the easiest part of the job first, then the other parts one at a time, in order of their difficulty, as the employee masters the easier parts

12. After an employee has completed telling his supervisor about a grievance against a co-worker, the supervisor tells the employee that he will take action to remove the cause of the grievance.
    The action of the supervisor was

    A. *good* because ill feeling between subordinates interferes with proper performance
    B. *poor* because the supervisor should give both employees time to *cool off*
    C. *good* because grievances that appear petty to the supervisor are important to subordinates
    D. *poor* because the supervisor should tell the employee that he will investigate the matter before he comes to any conclusion

13. During work on an important project, one employee in a secretarial pool turns in several pages of typed copy, one page of which contains several errors.
    Of these four comments which her supervisor might possibly make, which one would be MOST constructive?

    A. "You did such a poor job on this; I'll have to have it done over."
    B. "You will have to do better more consistently than this if you want to be in charge of a secretarial pool yourself someday."
    C. "How come you made so many mistakes here? Your other pages were all right."
    D. "If my boss saw this, he'd be very displeased with you."

14. A supervisor has general supervision over a large, complex project with many employees. The work is subdivided among small units of employees, each with a senior clerk or senior stenographer in charge. At a staff meeting, after all work assignments have been made, the supervisor tells all the employees that they are to take orders only from their immediate supervisor and instructs them to let him know if any one else tries to give them orders.
    This instruction by the supervisor is

    A. *good* because it may prevent the issuance of orders by unauthorized persons which would interfere with the accomplishment of the assignment
    B. *poor* because employees should be instructed to take up such problems with their immediate supervisor

C. *good* because orders issued by immediate supervisors would be precise and directly related to the tasks of the assignments while those issued by others would not be
D. *poor* because it places upon all employees a responsibility which should not normally be theirs

15. A supervisor who is to direct a team of senior clerks and clerks and senior stenographers and stenographers in a complex project calls them together beforehand to inform them of the tasks each employee will perform on this job. Of the following, the CHIEF value of this action by the supervisor is that each member of this team will be able to

    A. work independently in the absence of the supervisor
    B. understand what he will do and how this will fit into the total picture
    C. share in the process of decision-making as an equal participant
    D. judge how well the plans for this assignment have been made

16. A supervisor who has both younger and older employees under his supervision may sometimes find that employee absenteeism seriously interferes with accomplishment of goals.
    Studies of such employee absenteeism have shown that the absences of employees

    A. under 35 years of age are usually unexpected and the absences of employees over 45 years of age are usually unnecessary
    B. of all age groups show the same characteristics as to length of absence
    C. under 35 years of age are for frequent, short periods while the absences of employees over 45 years of age are less frequent but of longer duration
    D. under 35 years of age are for periods of long duration and the absences of employees over 45 years of age are for periods of short duration

17. Suppose you have a long-standing procedure for getting a certain job done by your subordinates that is apparently a good one. Changes in some steps of the procedure are made from time to time to handle special problems that come up.
    For you to review this procedure periodically is desirable MAINLY because

    A. the system is working well
    B. checking routines periodically is a supervisor's chief responsibility
    C. subordinates may be confused as to how the procedure operates as a result of the changes made
    D. it is necessary to determine whether the procedure has become outdated or is in need of improvement

18. In conducting an interview, the BEST types of questions with which to begin the interview are those which the person interviewed is _____ to answer.

    A. willing and able
    B. willing but unable
    C. able to but unwilling
    D. unable and unwilling

19. In order to determine accurately a child's age, it is BEST for an interviewer to rely on

    A. the child's grade in school
    B. what the mother says
    C. birth records
    D. a library card

20. In his first interview with a new employee, it would be LEAST appropriate for a unit super-   20.____
    visor to

    A. find out the employee's preference for the several types of jobs to which he is able
       to assign him
    B. determine whether the employee will make good promotion material
    C. inform the employee of what his basic job responsibilities will be
    D. inquire about the employee's education and previous employment

21. If an interviewer takes care to phrase his questions carefully and precisely, the result will   21.____
    MOST probably be that

    A. he will be able to determine whether the person interviewed is being truthful
    B. the free flow of the interview will be lost
    C. he will get the information he wants
    D. he will ask stereotyped questions and narrow the scope of the interview

22. When, during an interview, is the person interviewed LEAST likely to be cautious about   22.____
    what he tells the interviewer?

    A. Shortly after the beginning when the questions normally suggest pleasant associa-
       tions to the person interviewed
    B. As long as the interviewer keeps his questions to the point
    C. At the point where the person interviewed gains a clear insight into the area being
       discussed
    D. When the interview appears formally ended and goodbyes are being said

23. In an interview held for the purpose of getting information from the person interviewed, it   23.____
    is sometimes desirable for the interviewer to repeat the answer he has received
    to a question.
    For the interviewer to rephrase such an answer in his own words is good practice
    MAINLY because it

    A. gives the interviewer time to make up his next question
    B. gives the person interviewed a chance to correct any possible misunderstanding
    C. gives the person interviewed the feeling that the interviewer considers his answer
       important
    D. prevents the person interviewed from changing his answer

24. There are several methods of formulating questions during an interview. The particular   24.____
    method used should be adapted to the interview problems presented by the person
    being questioned.
    Of the following methods of formulating questions during an interview, the ACCEPT-
    ABLE one is for the interviewer to ask questions which

    A. incorporate several items in order to allow a cooperative interviewee freedom to
       organize his statements
    B. are ambiguous in order to foil a distrustful interviewee
    C. suggest the correct answer in order to assist an interviewee who appears confused
    D. would help an otherwise unresponsive interviewee to become more responsive

25. For an interviewer to permit the person being interviewed to read the data the interviewer writes as he records the person's responses on a routine departmental form is

    A. *desirable* because it serves to assure the person interviewed that his responses are being recorded accurately
    B. *undesirable* because it prevents the interviewer from clarifying uncertain points by asking additional questions
    C. *desirable* because it makes the time that the person interviewed must wait while the answer is written seem shorter
    D. *undesirable* because it destroys the confidentiality of the interview

26. Suppose that a stranger enters the office you are in charge of and asks for the address and telephone number of one of your employees.
    Of the following, it would be BEST for you to

    A. find out why he needs the information and release it if his reason is a good one
    B. explain that you are not permitted to release such information to unauthorized persons
    C. give him the information but tell him it must be kept confidential
    D. ask him to leave the office immediately

27. A member of the public approaches an employee who is at work at his desk. The employee cannot interrupt his work in order to take care of this person.
    Of the following, the BEST and MOST courteous way of handling this situation is for the employee to

    A. avoid looking up from his work until he is finished with what he is doing
    B. tell this person that he will not be able to take care of him for quite a while
    C. refer the individual to another employee who can take care of him right away
    D. chat with the individual while he continues with his work

28. You answer a phone call from a citizen who urgently needs certain information you do not have, but you think you know who may have it. He is angry because he has already been switched to two different offices.
    Of the following, it would be BEST for you to

    A. give him the phone number of the person you think may have the information he wants, but explain you are not sure
    B. tell him you regret you cannot help him because you are not sure who can give him the information
    C. advise him that the best way he can be sure of getting the information he wants is to write a letter to the agency
    D. get the phone number where he can be reached and tell him you will try to get the information he wants and will call him back later

29. Persons who have business with an agency often complain about the *red tape* which complicates or slows up what they are trying to accomplish.
    As a supervisor of a unit which deals with the public, the LEAST effective of the following actions which you could take to counteract this feeling on the part of a person who has business with your office is to

    A. assure him that your office will make every effort to take care of his matter as fast as possible
    B. tell him that because of the volume of work in your agency he must be patient with *red tape*

C. give him a reasonable date by which action on the matter he is concerned about will be completed and tell him to call you if he hasn't heard by then
D. give him an understanding of why the procedures he must comply with are necessary

30. If a receptionist is sorting letters at her desk and a caller appears to make an inquiry, the receptionist should

    A. ask the caller to have a seat and wait
    B. speak to the caller while continuing the sorting, looking up occasionally
    C. stop what she is doing and give undivided attention to the caller
    D. continue with the sorting until a logical break in the work is reached, then answer any inquiries

31. To avoid cutting off parts of letters when using an automatic letter opener, it is BEST to

    A. arrange all of the letters so that the addresses are right side up
    B. hold the envelopes up to the light to make sure their contents have not settled to the side that is to be opened
    C. strike the envelopes against a table or desk top several times so that the contents of all the envelopes settle to one side
    D. check the enclosures periodically to make sure that the machine has not been cutting into them

32. Requests to repair office equipment which appears to be unsafe should be given priority MAINLY because if repairs are delayed

    A. there may be injuries to staff
    B. there may be further deterioration of the equipment
    C. work flow may be interrupted
    D. the cost of repair may increase

33. Of the following types of documents, it is MOST important to retain and file

    A. working drafts of reports that have been submitted in final form
    B. copies of letters of good will which conveyed a message that could not be handled by phone
    C. interoffice orders for materials which have been received and verified
    D. interoffice memoranda regarding the routing of standard forms

34. Of the following, the BEST reason for discarding certain material from office files would be that the

    A. files are crowded
    B. material in the files is old
    C. material duplicates information obtainable from other sources in the files
    D. material is referred to most often by employees in an adjoining office

35. Of the following, the BEST reason for setting up a partitioned work area for the typists in your office is that

    A. an uninterrupted flow of work among the typists will be possible
    B. complaints about ventilation and lighting will be reduced
    C. the first-line supervisor will have more direct control over the typists
    D. the noise of the typewriters will be less disturbing to other workers

36. Of the following, the MAIN factor contributing to the expense of maintaining an office procedure manual would be the

    A. infrequent use of the manual
    B. need to revise it regularly
    C. cost of looseleaf binders
    D. high cost of printing

37. From the viewpoint of use of a typewriter to fill in a form, the MOST important design factor to consider is

    A. standard spacing
    B. box headings
    C. serial numbering
    D. vertical guide lines

38. Out-of-date and seldom used records should be removed PERIODICALLY from the files because

    A. overall responsibility for records will be transferred to the person in charge of the central storage files
    B. duplicate copies of every record are not needed
    C. valuable filing space will be regained and the time needed to find a current record will be cut down
    D. worthwhile suggestions on improving the filing system will result whenever this is done

39. In a certain office, file folders are constantly being removed from the files for use by administrators. At the same time, new material is coming in to be filed in some of these folders.
    Of the following, the BEST way to avoid delays in filing of the new material and to keep track of the removed folders is to

    A. keep a sheet listing all folders removed from the file, who has them, and a follow-up date to check on their return; attach to this list new material received for filing
    B. put an *out* slip in the place of any file folder removed, telling what folder is missing, date removed, and who has it; file new material received at front of files
    C. put a temporary *out* folder in place of the one removed, giving title or subject, date removed, and who has it; put into this temporary folder any new material received
    D. keep a list of all folders removed and who has them; forward any new material received for filing while a folder is out to the person who has it

40. Folders labeled *Miscellaneous* should be used in an alphabetic filing system MAINLY to

    A. provide quick access to recent material
    B. avoid setting up individual folders for all infrequent correspondents
    C. provide temporary storage for less important documents
    D. temporarily hold papers which will not fit into already crowded individual folders

41. Suppose that one of the office machines in your unit is badly in need of replacement. Of the following, the MOST important reason for postponing immediate purchase of a new machine would be that

    A. a later model of the machine is expected on the market in a few months
    B. the new machine is more expensive than the old machine
    C. the operator of the present machine will have to be instructed by the manufacturer in the operation of the new machine
    D. the employee operating the old machine is not complaining

42. If the four steps listed below for processing records were given in logical sequence, the one that would be the THIRD step is:

    A. Coding the records, using a chart or classification system
    B. Inspecting the records to make sure they have been released for filing
    C. Preparing cross-reference sheets or cards
    D. Skimming the records to determine filing captions

43. The suggestion that memos or directives which circulate among subordinates be initialed by each employee is a

    A. *poor* one because, with modern copying machines, it should be possible to supply every subordinate with a copy of each message for his personal use
    B. *good* one because it relieves the supervisor of blame for the action of subordinates who have read and initialed the messages
    C. *poor* one because initialing the memo or directive is no guarantee that the subordinate has read the material
    D. *good* one because it can be used as a record by the supervisor to show that his subordinates have received the message and were responsible for reading it

44. Of the following, the MOST important reason for microfilming office records is to

    A. save storage space needed to keep records
    B. make it easier to get records when needed
    C. speed up the classification of information
    D. shorten the time which records must be kept

45. Your office filing cabinets have become so overcrowded that it is difficult to use the files. Of the following, the MOST desirable step for you to take FIRST to relieve this situation would be to

    A. assign your assistant to spend some time each day reviewing the material in the files and to give you his recommendations as to what material may be discarded
    B. discard all material which has been in the files more than a given number of years
    C. submit a request for additional filing cabinets in your next budget request
    D. transfer enough material to the central storage room of your agency to give you the amount of additional filing space needed

46. Of the following, the USUAL order of the subdivisions in a standard published report is:

    A. Table of contents, body of report, index, appendix
    B. Index, table of contents, body of report, appendix
    C. Index, body of report, table of contents, appendix
    D. Table of contents, body of report, appendix, index

47. The BEST type of pictorial illustration to show the approximate percentage breakdown of the titles of employees in a department would be the

    A. flow chart   B. bar graph
    C. organization chart   D. line graph

48. You are reviewing a draft, written by one of your subordinates, of a report that is to be distributed to every bureau and division of your department.
Which one of the following would be the LEAST desirable characteristic of such a report?

   A. It gives information, explanations, conclusions, and recommendations for which purpose it was written.
   B. There is sufficient objective data presented to substantiate the conclusions reached and the recommendations made by the writer.
   C. The writing style and opinions of the writer are persuasive enough to win over to its conclusions those who read the report, although little data is given in support.
   D. It will be understood easily by the people to whom it will be distributed.

49. According to accepted practice, a business letter is addressed to an organization but marked for the attention of a specific individual whenever the sender wants

   A. only the person to whose attention the letter is sent to read the letter
   B. the letter to be opened and taken care of by someone else in the organization of the person for whose attention it is marked is away
   C. a reply only from the specific individual
   D. to improve the appearance and balance of the letter in cases where the company address is a long one

50. Which one of the following would be an ACCEPTABLE way to end a business letter?

   A. Hoping you will find this information useful, I remain
   B. Yours for continuing service
   C. I hope this letter gives you the information you need
   D. Trusting this gives you the information you desire, I am

KEY (CORRECT ANSWERS)

1. A	11. B	21. C	31. C	41. A
2. D	12. D	22. D	32. A	42. A
3. A	13. C	23. B	33. D	43. D
4. B	14. B	24. D	34. C	44. A
5. C	15. B	25. A	35. D	45. A
6. B	16. C	26. B	36. B	46. D
7. D	17. D	27. C	37. A	47. B
8. C	18. A	28. D	38. C	48. C
9. A	19. C	29. B	39. C	49. B
10. A	20. B	30. C	40. B	50. C

TEST 2

DIRECTIONS: Each question or incomplete statement is followed by several suggested answers or completions. Select the one that BEST answers the question or completes the statement. *PRINT THE LETTER OF THE CORRECT ANSWER IN THE SPACE AT THE RIGHT.*

1. You are replying to a letter from an individual who asks for a pamphlet put out by your agency. The pamphlet is out of print. A new pamphlet with a different title, but dealing with the same subject, is available.
   Of the following, it would be BEST that your reply indicate that

   A. you cannot send him the pamphlet he requested because it is out of print
   B. the pamphlet he requested is out of print, but he may be able to find it in the public library
   C. the pamphlet he requested is out of print, but you are sending him a copy of your agency's new pamphlet on the same subject
   D. since the pamphlet he requested is out of print, you would advise him to ask his friends or business acquaintances if they have a copy of it

1.____

2. An angry citizen sends a letter to your agency claiming that your office sent him the wrong form and complaining about the general inefficiency of city workers. Upon checking, you find that an incorrect form was indeed sent to this person.
   In reply, you should

   A. admit the error, apologize briefly, and enclose the correct form
   B. send the citizen the correct form with a transmittal letter stating only that the form is enclosed
   C. send him the correct form without any comment
   D. advise the citizen that mistakes happen in every large organization and that you are enclosing the correct form

2.____

3. It has been suggested that the language level of a letter of reply written by a government employee be geared no higher than the probable educational level of the person to whom the letter is written.
   This suggestion is a

   A. *good* one because it is easier for anyone to write letters simply, and this will make for a better reply
   B. *poor* one because it is not possible to judge, from one letter, the exact educational level of the writer
   C. *good* one because it will contribute to the recipient's comprehension of the contents of the letter
   D. *poor* one because the language should be at the simplest possible level so that anyone who reads the letter can understand it

3.____

4. Suppose that a large bureau has 187 employees. On a particular day, approximately 14% of these employees are not available for work because of absences due to vacation, illness, or other reasons. Of the remaining employees, 1/7 are assigned to a special project while the balance are assigned to the normal work of the bureau.
   The number of employees assigned to the normal work of the bureau on that day is

   A. 112   B. 124   C. 138   D. 142

4.____

5. Suppose that you are in charge of a typing pool of 8 typists. Two typists type at the rate of 38 words per minute; three type at the rate of 40 words per minute; three type at the rate of 42 words per minute. The average typewritten page consists of 50 lines, 12 words per line. Each employee works from 9 to 5 with one hour off for lunch.
   The total number of pages typed by this pool in one day is, on the average, CLOSEST to _____ pages.

   A. 205   B. 225   C. 250   D. 275

6. Suppose that part-time workers are paid $14.40 an hour, prorated to the nearest half hour, with pay guaranteed for a minimum of four hours if services are required for less than four hours. In one operation, part-time workers signed the time sheet as follows:

Worker	In	Out
A	8:00 A.M.	11:35 A.M.
B	8:30 A.M.	3:20 P.M.
C	7:55 A.M.	11:00 A.M.
D	8:30 A.M.	2:25 P.M.

   How much would total payment to these part-time workers amount to for this operation, assuming that those who stayed after 12 Noon were not paid for one hour which they took off for lunch?

   A. $268.80   B. $273.60   C. $284.40   D. $297.60

7. He wanted to *ascertain* the facts before arriving at a conclusion.
   The word *ascertain* means MOST NEARLY

   A. disprove   B. determine   C. convert   D. provide

8. Did the supervisor *assent* to her request for annual leave? The word *assent* means MOST NEARLY

   A. allude   B. protest   C. agree   D. refer

9. The new worker was fearful that the others would *rebuff* her.
   The word *rebuff* means MOST NEARLY

   A. ignore   B. forget   C. copy   D. snub

10. The supervisor of that office does not *condone* lateness. The word *condone* means MOST NEARLY

    A. mind   B. excuse   C. punish   D. remember

11. Each employee was instructed to be as *concise* as possible when preparing a report.
    The word *concise* means MOST NEARLY

    A. exact   B. sincere   C. flexible   D. brief

Questions 12-21.

DIRECTIONS: Below are 10 sentences numbered 12 to 21. Some of the sentences contain an error in spelling, word usage, or sentence structure, or punctuation. Some sentences are correct as they stand, although there may be other correct ways of expressing the same thought. All incorrect sentences contain only one error. Mark your answer to each question as follows:

A. if the sentence has an error in spelling
B. if the sentence has an error in punctuation or capitalization
C. if the sentence has an error in word usage or sentence structure
D. if the sentence is correct

12. Because the chairman failed to keep the participants from wandering off into irrelevant discussions, it was impossible to reach a consensus before the meeting was adjourned. 12._____

13. Certain employers have an unwritten rule that any applicant, who is over 55 years of age, is automatically excluded from consideration for any position whatsoever. 13._____

14. If the proposal to build schools in some new apartment buildings were to be accepted by the builders, one of the advantages that could be expected to result would be better communication between teachers and parents of schoolchildren. 14._____

15. In this instance, the manufacturer's violation of the law against deseptive packaging was discernible only to an experienced inspector. 15._____

16. The tenants' anger stemmed from the president's going to Washington to testify without consulting them first. 16._____

17. Did the president of this eminent banking company say; "We intend to hire and train a number of these disad-vantaged youths?" 17._____

18. In addition, today's confidential secretary must be knowledgable in many different areas: for example, she must know modern techniques for making travel arrangements for the executive. 18._____

19. To avoid further disruption of work in the offices, the protesters were forbidden from entering the building unless they had special passes. 19._____

20. A valuable secondary result of our training conferences is the opportunities afforded for management to observe the reactions of the participants. 20._____

21. Of the two proposals submitted by the committee, the first one is the best. 21._____

Questions 22-26.

DIRECTIONS: In Questions 22 through 26, choose the sentence which is BEST from the point of view of English usage suitable for a business letter or report.

22. A. It is the opinion of the Commissioners that programs which include the construction of cut-rate municipal garages in the central business district is inadvisable. 22._____
    B. Having reviewed the material submitted, the program for putting up cut-rate garages in the central business district seemed likely to cause traffic congestion.
    C. The Commissioners believe that putting up cut-rate municipal garages in the central business district is inadvisable.
    D. Making an effort to facilitate the cleaning of streets in the central business district, the building of cut-rate municipal garages presents the problem that it would encourage more motorists to come into the central city.

23. A. This letter, together with the reports, are to be sent to the principal.
     B. The reports, together with this letter, is to be sent to the principal.
     C. The reports and this letter is to be sent to the principal.
     D. This letter, together with the reports, is to be sent to the principal.

24. A. Each employee has to decide for themselves whether to take the examination.
     B. Each of the employees has to decide for himself whether to take the examination.
     C. Each of the employees has to decide for themselves whether to take the examination.
     D. Each of the employees have to decide for himself whether to take the examination.

25. A. The reason a new schedule is being prepared is that there has been a change in priorities.
     B. Because there has been a change in priorities is the reason why a new schedule is being made up.
     C. The reason why a new schedule is being made up is because there has been a change in priorities.
     D. Because of a change in priorities is the reason why a new schedule is being prepared.

26. A. The changes in procedure had an unfavorable affect upon the output of the unit.
     B. The increased output of the unit was largely due to the affect of the procedural changes.
     C. The changes in procedure had the effect of increasing the output of the unit.
     D. The increased output of the unit from the procedural changes were the effect.

Questions 27-33.

DIRECTIONS: Questions 27 through 33 are to be answered SOLELY on the basis of the information in the following extract, which is from a report prepared for Department X, which outlines the procedure to be followed in the case of transfers of employees.

Every transfer, regardless of the reason therefor, requires completion of the record of transfer, Form DT 411. To denote consent to the transfer, DT 411 should contain the signatures of the transferee and the personnel officer(s) concerned, except that, in the case of an involuntary transfer, the signatures of the transferee's present and prospective supervisors shall be entered in Boxes 8A and 8B, respectively, since the transferee does not consent. Only a permanent employee may request a transfer; in such cases, the employee's attendance record shall be duly considered with regard to absences, latenesses, and accrued overtime balances. In the case of an inter-district transfer, the employee's attendance record must be included in Section 8A of the transfer request, Form DT 410, by the personnel officer of the district from which the transfer is requested. The personnel officer of the district to which the employee requested transfer may refuse to accept accrued overtime balances in excess of ten days.

An employee on probation shall be eligible for transfer. If such employee is involuntarily transferred, he shall be credited for the period of time already served on probation. However, if such transfer is voluntary, the employee shall be required to serve the entire period of his probation in the new position. An employee who has occurred a disability which prevents him from performing his normal duties may be transferred during the period of such disability to other appropriate duties. A disability transfer requires the completion of either Form DT414 if the disability is job-connected, or Form DT 415 if it is not a job-connected disability. In either case, the personnel officer of the district from which the transfer is made signs in Box 6A of the first two copies and the personnel officer of the district to which the transfer is made signs in Box 6B of the last two copies; or, in the case of an intra-district disability transfer, the personnel officer must sign in Box 6A of the first two copies and Box 6B of the last two copies

27. When a personnel officer consents to an employee's request for transfer from his district, this procedure requires that the personnel officer sign Form(s)

    A. DT 411
    B. DT 410 and DT 411
    C. DT 411 and either Form DT 414 or DT 415
    D. DT 410 and DT 411, and either Form DT 414 or DT 415

28. With respect to the time record of an employee transferred against his wishes during his probationary period, this procedure requires that

    A. he serve the entire period of his probation in his present office
    B. he lose his accrued overtime balance
    C. his attendance record be considered with regard to absences and latenesses
    D. he be given credit for the period of time he has already served on probation

29. Assume you are a supervisor and an employee must be transferred into your office against his wishes.
    According to this procedure, the box you must sign on the record of transfer is

    A. 6A   B. 8A   C. 6B   D. 8B

30. Under this procedure, in the case of a disability transfer, when must Box 6A on Forms DT 414 and DT 415 be signed by the personnel officer of the district to which the transfer is being made?

    A. In all cases when either Form DT 414 or Form DT 415 is used
    B. In all cases when Form DT 414 is used and only under certain circumstances when Form DT 415 is used
    C. In all cases when Form DT 415 is used and only under certain circumstances when Form DT 414 is used
    D. Only under certain circumstances when either Form DT 414 or Form DT 415 is used

31. From the above passage, it may be inferred MOST correctly that the number of copies of Form DT 414 is

    A. no more than 2
    B. at least 3
    C. at least 5
    D. more than the number of copies of Form DT 415

32. A change in punctuation and capitalization only which would change one sentence into two and possibly contribute to somewhat greater ease of reading of this report extract would be MOST appropriate in the _____ sentence, _____ paragraph.

    A. 2nd; 1st
    B. 3rd; 1st
    C. next to the last; 2nd
    D. 2nd; 2nd

33. In the second paragraph, a word that is INCORRECTLY used is _____ in the _____ sentence.

    A. *shall;* 1st
    B. *voluntary;* 3rd
    C. *occurred;* 4th
    D. *intra-district;* last

Questions 34-38.

DIRECTIONS: Questions 34 through 38 are to be answered SOLELY on the basis of the information contained in the following passage.

Positive discipline minimizes the amount of personal supervision required and aids in the maintenance of standards. When a new employee has been properly introduced and carefully instructed, when he has come to know the supervisor and has confidence in the supervisor's ability to take care of him, when he willingly cooperates with the supervisor, that employee has been under positive discipline and can be put on his own to produce the quantity and quality of work desired. Negative discipline, the fear of transfer to a less desirable location, for example, to a limited extent may restrain certain individuals from overt violation of rules and regulations governing attendance and conduct which in governmental agencies are usually on at least an agency-wide basis. Negative discipline may prompt employees to perform according to certain rules to avoid a penalty such as, for example, docking for tardiness.

34. According to the above passage, it is reasonable to assume that in the area of discipline, the first-line supervisor in a governmental agency has GREATER scope for action in

    A. *positive* discipline because negative discipline is largely taken care of by agency rules and regulations
    B. *negative* discipline because rules and procedures are already fixed and the supervisor can rely on them
    C. *positive* discipline because the supervisor is in a position to recommend transfers
    D. *negative* discipline because positive discipline is reserved for people on a higher supervisory level

35. In order to maintain positive discipline of employees under his supervision, it is MOST important for a supervisor to

    A. assure each employee that he has nothing to worry about
    B. insist at the outset on complete cooperation from employees
    C. be sure that each employee is well trained in his job
    D. inform new employees of the penalties for not meeting standards

36. According to the above passage, a feature of negative discipline is that it

    A. may lower employee morale
    B. may restrain employees from disobeying the rules
    C. censures equal treatment of employees
    D. tends to create standards for quality of work

37. A REASONABLE conclusion based on the above passage is that positive discipline benefits a supervisor because

    A. he can turn over orientation and supervision of a new employee to one of his subordinates
    B. subordinates learn to cooperate with one another when working on an assignment
    C. it is easier to administer
    D. it cuts down, in the long run, on the amount of time the supervisor needs to spend on direct supervision

38. Based on the above passage, it is REASONABLE to assume that an important difference between positive discipline and negative discipline is that positive discipline

    A. is concerned with the quality of work and negative discipline with the quantity of work
    B. leads to a more desirable basis for motivation of the employee
    C. is more likely to be concerned with agency rules and regulations
    D. uses fear while negative discipline uses penalties to prod employees to adequate performance

Questions 39-50.

DIRECTIONS: Questions 39 through 50 are to be answered on the basis of the information given in the graph and chart below.

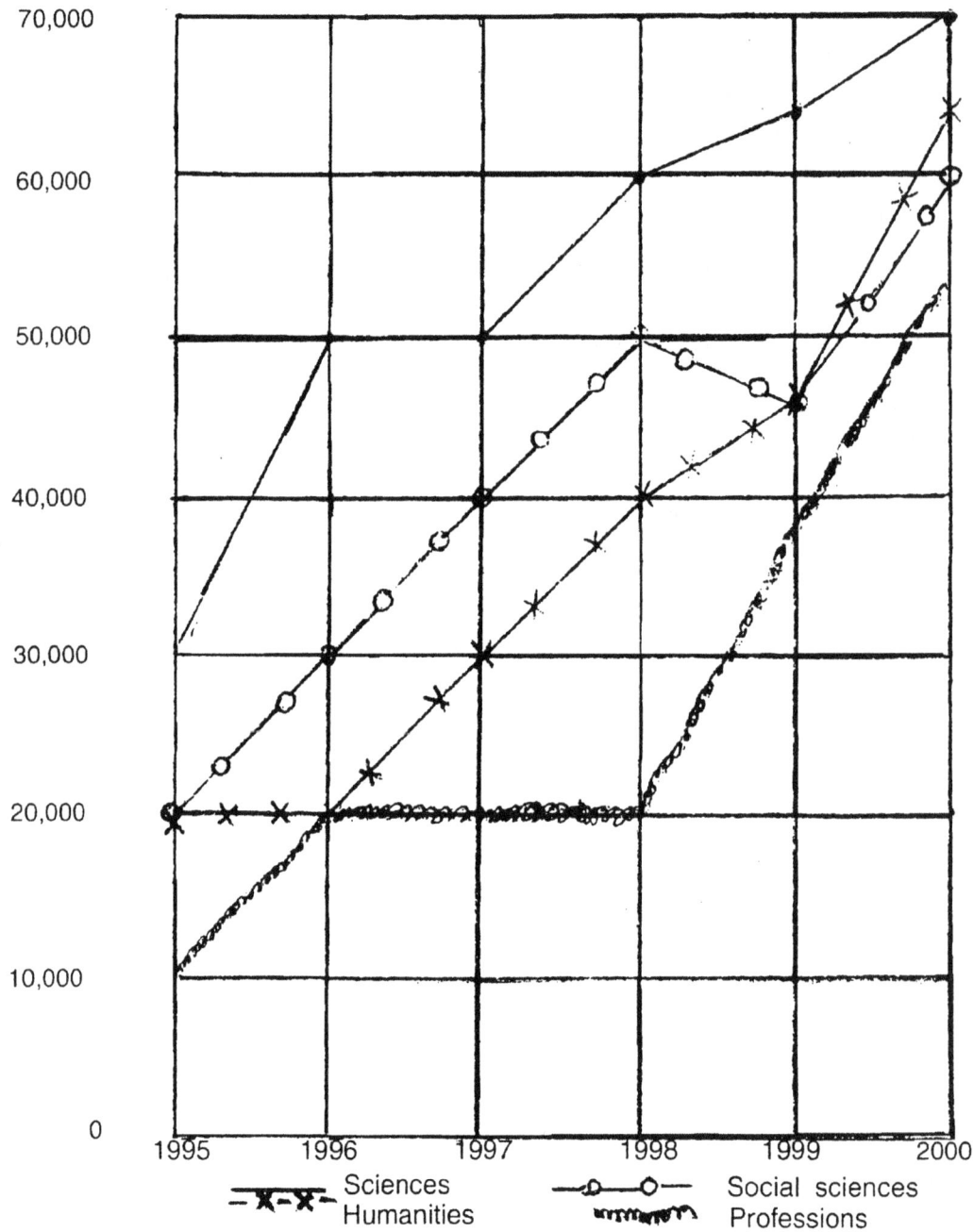

ENROLLMENT IN POSTGRADUATE STUDIES

Fields	Subdivisions	1999	2000
Sciences	Math	10,000	12,000
	Physical science	22,000	24,000
	Behavioral science	32,000	35,000
Humanities	Literature	26,000	34,000
	Philosophy	6,000	8,000
	Religion	4,000	6,000
	Arts	10,000	16,000
Social sciences	History	36,000	46,000
	Sociology	8,000	14,000
Professions	Law	2,000	2,000
	Medicine	6,000	8,000
	Business	30,000	44,000

39. The number of students enrolled in the social sciences and in the humanities was the same in _____ and _____.

    A. 1997; 1999
    B. 1995; 1999
    C. 1999; 2000
    D. 1996; 1999

40. A comparison of the enrollment of students in the various postgraduate studies shows that in every year from 1995 through 2000, there were more students enrolled in the _____ than in the _____.

    A. professions; sciences
    B. humanities; professions
    C. social sciences; professions
    D. humanities; sciences

41. The number of students enrolled in the humanities was GREATER than the number of students enrolled in the professions by the same amount in _____ of the years.

    A. two   B. three   C. four   D. five

42. The one field of postgraduate study to show a decrease in enrollment in one year compared to the year immediately preceding is

    A. humanities
    B. sciences
    C. professions
    D. social sciences

43. If the proportion of arts students to all humanities students was the same in 1997 as in 2000, then the number of arts students in 1997 was

    A. 7,500   B. 13,000   C. 15,000   D. 5,000

44. In which field of postgraduate study did enrollment INCREASE by 20 percent from 1997 to 1998?

    A. Humanities
    B. Professions
    C. Sciences
    D. Social sciences

45. The GREATEST increase in overall enrollment took place between

    A. 1995 and 1996
    B. 1997 and 1998
    C. 1998 and 1999
    D. 1999 and 2000

46. Between 1997 and 2000, the combined enrollment of the sciences and social sciences increased by

    A. 40,000   B. 48,000   C. 50,000   D. 54,000

47. If the enrollment in the social sciences had decreased from 1999 to 2000 at the same rate as from 1998 to 1999, then the social science enrollment in 2000 would have differed from the humanities enrollment in 2000 MOST NEARLY by

    A. 6,000   B. 8,000   C. 12,000   D. 22,000

48. In the humanities, the GREATEST percentage increase in enrollment from 1999 to 2000 was in

    A. literature   B. philosophy
    C. religion   D. arts

49. If the proportion of behavioral science students to the total number of students in the sciences was the same in 1996 as in 1999, then the increase in behavioral science enrollment from 1996 to 2000 was

    A. 5,000   B. 7,000   C. 10,000   D. 14,000

50. If enrollment in the professions increased at the same rate from 2000 to 2001 as from 1999 to 2000, the enrollment in the professions in 2001 would be MOST NEARLY

    A. 85,000   B. 75,000   C. 60,000   D. 55,000

KEY (CORRECT ANSWERS)

1. C	11. D	21. C	31. B	41. B
2. A	12. C	22. C	32. B	42. D
3. C	13. B	23. D	33. C	43. A
4. C	14. D	24. B	34. A	44. C
5. B	15. A	25. A	35. C	45. D
6. B	16. D	26. C	36. B	46. A
7. B	17. B	27. A	37. D	47. D
8. C	18. A	28. D	38. B	48. D
9. D	19. C	29. D	39. B	49. C
10. B	20. D	30. D	40. C	50. B

EXAMINATION SECTION

TEST 1

DIRECTIONS: Each question or incomplete statement is followed by several suggested answers or completions. Select the one that BEST answers the question or completes the statement. *PRINT THE LETTER OF THE CORRECT ANSWER IN THE SPACE AT THE RIGHT.*

Questions 1-4.

DIRECTIONS: Questions 1 through 4 are to be answered SOLELY on the basis of the following passage.

Job analysis combined with performance appraisal is an excellent method of determining training needs of individuals. The steps in this method are to determine the specific duties of the job, to evaluate the adequacy with which the employee performs each of these duties, and finally to determine what significant improvements can be made by training.

The list of duties can be obtained in a number of ways: asking the employee, asking the supervisor, observing the employee, etc. Adequacy of performance can be estimated by the employee, but the supervisor's evaluation must also be obtained. This evaluation will usually be based on observation.

What does the supervisor observe? The employee, while he is working; the employee's work relationships; the ease, speed, and sureness of the employee's actions; the way he applies himself to the job; the accuracy and amount of completed work; its conformity with established procedures and standards; the appearance of the work; the soundness of judgment it shows; and, finally, signs of good or poor communication, understanding, and cooperation among employees.

Such observation is a normal and inseparable part of the everyday job of supervision. Systematically, recorded, evaluated, and summarized, it highlights both general and individual training needs.

1. According to the passage, job analysis may be used by the supervisor in   1.____
   A. increasing his own understanding of tasks performed in his unit
   B. increasing efficiency of communication within the organization
   C. assisting personnel experts in the classification of positions
   D. determining in which areas an employee needs more instruction

2. According to the passage, the FIRST step in determining the training needs of   2.____
   employees is to
   A. locate the significant improvements that can be made by training
   B. determine the specific duties required in a job
   C. evaluate the employee's performance
   D. motivate the employee to want to improve himself

3. On the basis of the above passage, which of the following is the BEST way for a supervisor to determine the adequacy of employee performance?
   A. Check the accuracy and amount of completed work
   B. Ask the training officer
   C. Observe all aspects of the employee's work
   D. Obtain the employee's own estimate

4. Which of the following is NOT mentioned by the passage as a factor to be taken into consideration in judging the adequacy of employee performance?
   A. Accuracy of completed work
   B. Appearance of completed work
   C. Cooperation among employees
   D. Attitude of the employee toward his supervisor

5. In indexing names of business firms and other organizations, ONE of the rules to be followed is:
   A. The word *and* is considered an indexing unit.
   B. When a firm name includes the full name of a person who is not well-known, the person's first name is considered as the first indexing unit.
   C. Usually the units in a firm name are indexed in the order in which they are written.
   D. When a firm's name is made up of single letters (such as ABC Corp.), the letters taken together are considered more than one indexing unit.

6. Assume that people often come to your office with complaints of errors in your agency's handling of their clients. The employees in your office have the job of listening to these complaints and investigating them. One day, when it is almost closing time, a person comes into your office, apparently very angry, and demands that you take care of his complaint at once.
   Your IMMEDIATE reaction should be to
   A. suggest that he return the following day
   B. find out his name and the nature of his complaint
   C. tell him to write a letter
   D. call over your supervisor

7. Assume that part of your job is to notify people concerning whether their applications for a certain program have been approved or disapproved. However, you do not actually make the decision on approval or disapproval. One day, you answer a telephone call from a woman who states that she has not yet received any word on her application. She goes on to tell you her qualifications for the program. From what she has said, you know that persons with such qualifications are usually approved.
   Of the following, which one is the BEST thing for you to say to her?
   A. "You probably will be accepted, but wait until you receive a letter before trying to join the program."
   B. "Since you seem well qualified, I am sure that your application will be approved."

C. "If you can write us a letter emphasizing your qualifications, it may speed up the process."
D. "You will be notified of the results of your application as soon as a decision has been made."

8. Suppose that one of your duties includes answering specific telephone inquiries. Your superior refers a call to you from an irate person who claims that your agency is inefficient and is wasting taxpayers' money.
Of the following, the BEST way to handle such a call is to
   A. listen briefly and then hang up without answering
   B. note the caller's comments and tell him that you will transmit them to your superiors
   C. connect the caller with the head of your agency
   D. discuss your own opinions with the caller

8.____

9. An employee has been assigned to open her division head's mail and place it on his desk. One day, the employee opens a letter which she then notices is marked *Personal*.
Of the following, the BEST action for her to take is to
   A. write *Personal* on the letter and staple the envelope to the back of the letter
   B. ignore the matter and treat the letter the same way as the others
   C. give it to another division head to hold until her own division head comes into the office
   D. leave the letter in the envelope and write *Sorry opened by mistake* on the envelope and initial it

9.____

Questions 10-14.

DIRECTIONS: Questions 10 through 14 each consist of a quotation which contains one word that is incorrectly used because it is not in keeping with the meaning that the quotation is evidently intended to convey. Of the words underlined in each quotation, determine which word is incorrectly used. Then select from among the words lettered A, B, C, and D the word which, when substituted for the incorrectly used word, would BEST help to convey the meaning of the quotation. (Do not indicate a change for an underlined word unless the underlined word is incorrectly used.)

10. Unless reasonable managerial supervision is <u>exercised</u> over office supplies, it is certain that there will be extravagance, <u>rejected</u> items out of stock, <u>excessive</u> prices paid for certain items, and <u>obsolete</u> material in the stockroom.
    A. overlooked   B. immoderate   C. needed   D. instituted

10.____

11. Since <u>office</u> supplies are in such <u>common</u> use, an attitude of indifference about their handling is not <u>unusual</u>. Their importance is often recognized only when they are <u>utilized</u> or out of stock, for office employees must have proper supplies if maximum productivity is to be <u>attained</u>.
    A. plentiful   B. unavailable   C. reduced   D. expected

11.____

12. Anyone <u>effected</u> by paperwork, <u>interested</u> in or engaged in office work, or desiring to improve <u>informational</u> activities can find materials <u>keyed</u> to his needs.
    A. attentive   B. available   C. affected   D. ambitious

13. Information is <u>homogeneous</u> and must therefore be properly classified so that each type may be <u>employed</u> in ways <u>appropriate</u> to its <u>own peculiar</u> properties.
    A. apparent
    B. heterogeneous
    C. consistent
    D. idiosyncratic

14. <u>Intellectual</u> training may seem a <u>formidable</u> phrase, but it means nothing more than the <u>deliberate</u> cultivation of the ability to think, and there is no <u>dark</u> contrast between the intellectual and the practical.
    A. subjective   B. objective   C. sharp   D. vocational

15. The MOST important reason for having a filing system is to
    A. get papers out of the way
    B. have a record of everything that has happened
    C. retain information to justify your actions
    D. enable rapid retrieval of information

16. The system of filing which is used MOST frequently is called _____ filing.
    A. alphabetic
    B. alphanumeric
    C. geographic
    D. numeric

17. One of the clerks under your supervision has been telephoning frequently to tell you that he was taking the day off. Unless there is a real need for it, taking leave which is not scheduled is frowned upon because it upsets the work schedule.
    Under these circumstances, which of the following reasons for taking the day off is MOST acceptable?
    A. "I can't work when my arthritis bothers me."
    B. "I've been pressured with work from my night job and needed the extra time to catch up."
    C. "My family just moved to a new house, and I needed the time to start the repairs."
    D. "Work here has not been challenging, and I've been looking for another job."

18. One of the employees under your supervision, previously a very satisfactory worker, has begun arriving late one or two mornings each week. No explanation has been offered for this change. You call her to your office for a conference. As you are explaining the purpose of the conference and your need to understand this sudden lateness problem, she becomes very angry and states that you have no right to question her.
    Of the following, the BEST course of action for you to take at this point is to

5 (#1)

    A. inform her in your most authoritarian tone that you are the supervisor and that you have every right to question her
    B. end the conference and advise the employee that you will have no further discussion with her until she controls her temper
    C. remain calm, try to calm her down, and when she has quieted, explain the reasons for your questions and the need for answers
    D. hold your temper; when she has calmed down, tell her that you will not have a tardy worker in your unit and will have her transferred at once

19. Assume that, in the branch of the agency for which you work, you are the only clerical person on the staff with a supervisory title and, in addition, that you are the office manager. On a particular day when all members of the professional staff are away from the building attending an important meeting, an urgent call comes through requesting some confidential information ordinarily released only by professional staff.
Of the following, the MOST reasonable action for you to take is to
    A. decline to give the information because you are not a member of the professional staff
    B. offer to call back after you get permission from the agency director at the main office
    C. advise the caller that you will supply the information as soon as your chief returns
    D. supply the information requested and inform your chief when she returns

20. As a supervisor, you are scheduled to attend an important conference with your superior. However, that day you learn that your very capable assistant is ill and unable to come to work. Several highly sensitive tasks are scheduled for completion on this day.
Of the following, the BEST way to handle this situation is to
    A. tell your supervisor you cannot attend the meeting and ask that it be postponed
    B. assign one of your staff to see that the jobs are completed and turned in
    C. advise your supervisor of the situation and ask what you should do
    D. call the departments for which the work is being done and ask for an extension of time

21. When a decision needs to be made which is likely to affect units other than his own, a supervisor should USUALLY
    A. make such a decision quickly and then discuss it with his supervisor
    B. make such a decision only after careful consultation with his subordinates
    C. discuss the problem with his immediate superior before making such a decision
    D. have his subordinates arrive at such a decision in conference with the subordinates in the other units

22. Assume that, as a supervisor in Division X, you are training Ms. Y, a new employee, to answer the telephone properly.
You should explain that the BEST way to answer is to pick up the receiver and say:

A. "What is your name, please?" B. "May I help you?"
C. "Ms. Y speaking." D. "Division X, Ms. Y speaking."

Questions 23-25.

DIRECTIONS: Questions 23 through 25 consist of sentences in which two words are missing. Examine each sentence, and then choose from below it the words which should be inserted in the blank spaces in order to create a coherent and well-written sentence.

23. Human behavior is far _____ variable, and therefore _____ predictable, than that of any other species.   23._____
    A. less; as   B. less; not   C. more; not   D. more; less

24. The _____ limitation of this method is that the results are based _____ a narrow sample.   24._____
    A. chief; with   B. chief; on   C. only; for   D. only; to

25. Although there _____ a standard procedure for handling these problems, each case often has _____ own unique features.   25._____
    A. are; its   B. are; their   C. is; its   D. is; their

KEY (CORRECT ANSWERS)

1.	D	11.	B
2.	B	12.	C
3.	C	13.	B
4.	D	14.	C
5.	C	15.	D
6.	B	16.	A
7.	D	17.	A
8.	B	18.	C
9.	D	19.	B
10.	C	20.	C

21. C
22. D
23. D
24. B
25. C

TEST 2

DIRECTIONS: Each question or incomplete statement is followed by several suggested answers or completions. Select the one that BEST answers the question or completes the statement. *PRINT THE LETTER OF THE CORRECT ANSWER IN THE SPACE AT THE RIGHT.*

Questions 1-3.

DIRECTIONS: Questions 1 through 3 each consist of a group of four sentences. Read each sentence carefully, and select the one of the four in each group which represents the BEST English usage for business letters and reports.

1. A. The chairman himself, rather than his aides, has reviewed the report.
   B. The chairman himself, rather than his aides, have reviewed the report.
   C. The chairmen, not the aide, has reviewed the report.
   D. The aide, not the chairmen, have reviewed the report.

    1.____

2. A. Various proposals were submitted but the decision is not been made.
   B. Various proposals has been submitted but the decision has not been made.
   C. Various proposals were submitted but the decision is not been made.
   D. Various proposals have been submitted but the decision has not been made.

    2.____

3. A. Everyone were rewarded for his successful attempt.
   B. They were successful in their attempts and each of them was rewarded.
   C. Each of them are rewarded for their successful attempts.
   D. The reward for their successful attempts were made to each of them.

    3.____

4. Which of the following is MOST suited to arrangement in chronological order?
    A. Applications for various types and levels of jobs
    B. Issues of a weekly publication
    C. Weekly time cards for all employees for the week of April 21
    D. Personnel records for all employees

    4.____

5. Words that are *synonymous* with a given word ALWAYS _____ the given word.
    A. have the same meaning as   B. have the same pronunciation as
    C. have the opposite meaning of   D. can be rhymed with

    5.____

Questions 6-11.

DIRECTIONS: Questions 6 through 11 are to be answered on the basis of the following chart showing numbers of errors made by four clerks in one work unit for a half-year period.

47

	Allan	Barry	Cary	David
July	5	4	1	7
August	8	3	9	8
September	7	8	7	5
October	3	6	5	3
November	2	4	4	6
December	5	2	8	4

6. The clerk with the HIGHEST number of errors for the six-month period was
    A. Allan   B. Barry   C. Cary   D. David

    6.____

7. If the number of errors made by Allan in the six months shown represented one-eighth of the total errors made by the unit during the entire year, what was the TOTAL number of errors made by the unit for the year?
    A. 124   B. 180   C. 240   D. 360

    7.____

8. The number of errors made by David in November was what FRACTION of the total errors made in November?
    A. 1/3   B. 1/6   C. 3/8   D. 3/16

    8.____

9. The average number of errors made per month per clerk was MOST NEARLY
    A. 4   B. 5   C. 6   D. 7

    9.____

10. Of the total number of errors made during the six-month period, the percentage made in August was MOST NEARLY
    A. 2%   B. 4%   C. 23%   D. 4%

    10.____

11. If the number of errors in the unit were to decrease in the next six months by 30%, what would be MOST NEARLY the total number of errors for the unit for the next six months?
    A. 87   B. 94   C. 120   D. 137

    11.____

12. The arithmetic mean salary for five employees earning $18,500, $18,300, $18,600, $18,400, and $18,500, respectively is
    A. $18,450   B. $18,460   C. $18,475   D. $18,500

    12.____

13. Last year, a city department which is responsible for purchasing supplies ordered bond paper in equal quantities from 22 different companies. The price was exactly the same for each company, and the total cost for the 22 orders was $693,113.
    Assuming prices did not change during the year, the cost of EACH order was MOST NEARLY
    A. $31,490   B. $31,495   C. $31,500   D. $31,505

    13.____

14. A city agency engaged in repair work uses a small part which the city purchases for $0.14 each. Assume that, in a certain year, the total expenditure of the city for this part was $700.
    How MANY of these parts were purchased that year?
    A. 50   B. 200   C. 2,000   D. 5,000

15. The work unit which you supervise is responsible for processing fifteen reports per month.
    If your unit has four clerks and the best worker completes 40% of the reports himself, how many reports would each of the other clerks have to complete if they all do an equal number?
    A. 1   B. 2   C. 3   D. 4

16. Assume that the work unit in which you work has 24 clerks and 18 stenographers. In order to change the ratio of stenographers to clerks so that there is one stenographer for every four clerks, it would be necessary to REDUCE the number of stenographers by
    A. 3   B. 6   C. 9   D. 12

17. Assume that your office is responsible for opening and distributing all the mail of the division. After opening a letter, one of your subordinates notices that it states that there should be an enclosure in the envelope. However, there is no enclosure in the envelope.
    Of the following, the BEST instruction that you can give the clerk is to
    A. call the sender to obtain the enclosure
    B. call the addressee to inform him that the enclosure is missing
    C. note the omission in the margin of the letter
    D. forward the letter without taking any action

18. While opening the envelope containing official correspondence, you accidentally cut the enclosed letter.
    Of the following, the BEST action for you to take is to
    A. leave the material as it is
    B. put it together by using transparent mending tape
    C. keep it together by putting it back in the envelope
    D. keep it together by using paper clips

19. Suppose your supervisor is on the telephone in his office and an applicant arrives for a scheduled interview with him.
    Of the following, the BEST procedure to follow ordinarily is to
    A. informally chat with the applicant in your office until your supervisor has finished his phone conversation
    B. escort him directly into your supervisor's office and have him wait for him there
    C. inform your supervisor of the applicant's arrival and try to make the applicant feel comfortable while waiting
    D. have him hang up his coat and tell him to go directly in to see your supervisor

20. The length of time that files should be kept is GENERALLY
    A. considered to be seven years
    B. dependent upon how much new material has accumulated in the files
    C. directly proportionate to the number of years the office has been in operation
    D. dependent upon the type and nature of the material in the files

21. Cross-referencing a document when you file it means
    A. making a copy of the document and putting the copy into a related file
    B. indicating on the front of the document the name of the person who wrote it, the date it was written, and for what purpose
    C. putting a special sheet or card in a related file to indicate where the document is filed
    D. indicating on the document where it is to be filed

22. Unnecessary handling and recording of incoming mail could be eliminated by
    A. having the person who opens it initial it
    B. indicating on the piece of mail the names of all the individuals who should see it
    C. sending all incoming mail to more than one central location
    D. making a photocopy of each piece of incoming mail

23. Of the following, the office tasks which lend themselves MOST readily to planning and study are
    A. repetitive, occur in volume, and extend over a period of time
    B. cyclical in nature, have small volume, and extend over a short period of time
    C. tasks which occur only once in a great while not according to any schedule, and have large volume
    D. special tasks which occur only once, regardless of their volume and length of time

24. A good recordkeeping system includes all of the following procedures EXCEPT the
    A. filing of useless records
    B. destruction of certain files
    C. transferring of records from one type of file to another
    D. creation of inactive files

25. Assume that, as a supervisor, you are responsible for orienting and training new employees in your unit.
    Which of the following can MOST properly be omitted from your discussions with a new employee?
    A. The purpose of commonly used office forms
    B. Time and leave regulations
    C. Procedures for required handling of routine business calls
    D. The reason the last employee was fired

KEY (CORRECT ANSWERS)

1.	A	11.	A
2.	D	12.	B
3.	B	13.	D
4.	B	14.	D
5.	A	15.	C
6.	C	16.	D
7.	C	17.	C
8.	C	18.	B
9.	B	19.	C
10.	C	20.	D

21.	C
22.	B
23.	A
24.	A
25.	D

EXAMINATION SECTION
TEST 1

DIRECTIONS: Each question or incomplete statement is followed by several suggested answers or completions. Select the one that BEST answers the question or completes the statement. *PRINT THE LETTER OF THE CORRECT ANSWER IN THE SPACE AT THE RIGHT.*

1. Records of one type or another are kept in every office. The MOST important of the following reasons for the supervisor of a clerical or stenographic unit to keep statistical records of the work done in his unit is generally to

    A. supply basic information needed in planning the work of the unit
    B. obtain statistics for comparison with other units
    C. serve as the basis for unsatisfactory employee evaluation
    D. provide the basis for special research projects on program budgeting

    1._____

2. It is better for an employee to report and be responsible directly to several supervisors than to report and be responsible to only one supervisor.
This statement directly CONTRADICTS the supervisory principle generally known as

    A. span of control
    B. unity of command
    C. delegation of authority
    D. accountability

    2._____

3. The one of the following which would MOST likely lead to friction among clerks in a unit is for the unit supervisor to

    A. defend the actions of his clerks when discussing them with his own supervisor
    B. praise each of his clerks "in confidence" as the best clerk in the unit
    C. get his men to work together as a team in completing the work of the unit
    D. consider the point of view of the rank and file clerks when assigning unpleasant tasks

    3._____

4. You become aware that one of the employees you supervise has failed to follow correct procedure and has been permitting various reports to be prepared, typed, and transmitted improperly.
The BEST action for you to take FIRST in this situation is to

    A. order the employee to review all departmental procedures and reprimand him for having violated them
    B. warn the employee that he must obey regulations because uniformity is essential for effective departmental operation
    C. confer with the employee both about his failure to follow regulations and his reasons for doing so
    D. watch the employee's work very closely in the future but say nothing about this violation

    4._____

5. The supervisory clerk who would be MOST likely to have poor control over his subordinates is the one who

    A. goes to unusually great lengths to try to win their approval
    B. pitches in with the work they are doing during periods of heavy workload when no extra help can be obtained

    5._____

C. encourages and helps his subordinates toward advancement
D. considers suggestions from his subordinates before establishing new work procedures involving them

6. Suppose that a clerk who has been transferred to your office from another division in your agency because of difficulties with his supervisor has been placed under your supervision.
The BEST course of action for you to take FIRST is to

   A. instruct the clerk in the duties he will be performing in your office and make him feel "wanted" in his new position
   B. analyze the clerk's past grievance to determine if the transfer was the best solution to the problem
   C. advise him of the difficulties that his former supervisor had with other employees and encourage him not to feel badly about the transfer
   D. warn him that you will not tolerate any nonsense and that he will be under continuous surveillance while assigned to you

7. A certain office supervisor takes the initiative to represent his employees' interests related to working conditions, opportunities for advancement, etc. to his own supervisor and the administrative levels of the agency. This supervisor's actions will MOST probably have the effect of

   A. preventing employees from developing individual initiative in their work goals
   B. encouraging employees to compete openly for the special attention of their supervisor
   C. depriving employees of the opportunity to be represented by persons and/or unions of their own choosing
   D. building employee confidence in their supervisor and a spirit of cooperation in their work

8. Suppose that you have been promoted, assigned as a supervisor of a certain unit and asked to reorganize its functions so that specific routine procedures can be established. Before deciding which routines to establish, the FIRST of the following steps you should take is to

   A. decide who will perform each task in the routine
   B. determine the purpose to be served by each routine procedure
   C. outline the sequence of steps in each routine to be established
   D. calculate if more staff will be needed to carry out the new procedures

9. When routine procedures covering the ordinary work of an office are established, the supervisor of the office tends to be relieved of the need to

   A. make repeated decisions on the handling of recurring similar situations
   B. check the accuracy of the work completed by his subordinates
   C. train his subordinates in new work procedures
   D. plan and schedule the work of his office

10. Of the following, the method which would be LEAST helpful to a supervisor in effectively applying the principles of on-the-job safety to the daily work of his unit is for him to

A. initiate corrections of unsafe layouts of equipment and unsafe work processes
B. take charge of operations that are not routine to make certain that safety precautions are established and observed
C. continue to "talk safety" and promote safety consciousness in his subordinates
D. figure the cost of all accidents which could possibly occur on the job

11. A clerk is assigned to serve as receptionist for a large and busy office. Although many members of the public visit this office, the clerk often experiences periods of time in which he has nothing to do.
In these circumstances, the MOST advisable of the following actions for the supervisor to take is to

    A. assign a number of relatively low priority clerical jobs to the receptionist to do in the slow periods
    B. regularly rotate this assignment so that all the clerks experience this lighter work load
    C. assign the receptionist job as part of the duties of a number of clerks whose desks are nearest the reception room
    D. overlook the situation, since most of the receptionist's time is spent in performing a necessary and meaningful function

11._____

12. For a supervisor to require all stenographers in a stenographic pool to produce the same amount of work on a particular day is

    A. *advisable;* since it will prove that the supervisor plays no favorites
    B. *fair;* since all the stenographers are receiving approximately the same salary, their output should be equivalent
    C. *not necessary;* since the fast workers will compensate for the slow workers
    D. *not realistic;* since individual differences in abilities and work assignment must be taken into consideration

12._____

13. The establishment of a centralized typing pool to service the various units in an organization is MOST likely to be worthwhile when there is

    A. wide fluctuation from time to time in the needs of the various units for typing service
    B. a large volume of typing work to be done in each of the units
    C. a need by each unit for different kinds of typing service
    D. a training program in operation to develop and maintain typing skills

13._____

14. A newly appointed supervisor should learn as much as possible about the backgrounds of his subordinates. This statement is generally CORRECT because

    A. knowing their backgrounds assures they will be treated objectively, equally, and without favor
    B. effective handling of subordinates is based upon knowledge of their individual differences
    C. subordinates perform more efficiently under one supervisor than under another
    D. subordinates have confidence in a supervisor who knows all about them

14._____

15. The use of electronic computers in modern businesses has produced many changes in office and information management. Of the following, it would NOT be correct to state that computer utilization

15._____

A. broadens the scope of managerial and supervisory authority
B. establishes uniformity in the processing and reporting of information
C. cuts costs by reducing the personnel needed for efficient office operation
D. supplies management rapidly with up-to-date data to facilitate decision-making

16. The CHIEF advantage of having a single, large open office instead of small partitioned ones for a clerical unit or stenographic pool is that the single, large open office

    A. affords privacy without isolation for all office workers not directly dealing with the public
    B. assures the smoother, more continuous inter-office flow of work that is essential for efficient work production
    C. facilitates the office supervisor's visual control over and communication with his subordinates
    D. permits a more decorative and functional arrangement of office furniture and machines

17. When a supervisor provides a new employee with the information necessary for a basic knowledge and a general understanding of practices and procedures of the agency, he is applying the type of training generally known as _____ training.

    A. pre-employment   B. induction
    C. on-the-job   D. supervisory

18. Many government agencies require the approval by a central forms control unit of the design and reproduction of new office forms.
    The one of the following results of this procedure that is a DISADVANTAGE is that requiring prior approval of a central forms control unit USUALLY

    A. limits the distribution of forms to those offices with justifiable reasons for receiving them
    B. permits checking whether existing forms or modifications of them are in line with current agency needs
    C. encourages reliance on only the central office to set up all additional forms when needed
    D. provides for someone with a specialized knowledge of forms design to review and criticize new and revised forms

19. Suppose that a large quantity of information is in the files which are located a good distance from your desk. Almost every worker in your office must use these files constantly. Your duties in particular require that you daily refer to about 25 of the same items. They are short, one-page items distributed throughout the files.
    In this situation, your BEST course would be to

    A. take the items that you use daily from the files and keep them on your desk, inserting "out cards" in their place
    B. go to the files each time you need the information so that the items will be there when other workers need them
    C. make xerox copies of the information you use most frequently and keep them in your desk for ready reference
    D. label the items you use most often with different colored tabs for immediate identification

20. Of the following, the MOST important advantage of preparing manuals of office procedures in loose-leaf form is that this form

    A. permits several employees to use different sections simultaneously
    B. facilitates the addition of new material and the removal of obsolete material
    C. is more readily arranged in alphabetical order
    D. reduces the need for cross-references to locate material carried under several headings

21. Suppose that you establish a new clerical procedure for the unit you supervise. Your keeping a close check on the time required by your staff to handle the new procedure is wise MAINLY because such a check will find out

    A. whether your subordinates know how to handle the new procedure
    B. whether a revision of the unit's work schedule will be necessary as a result of the new procedure
    C. what attitude your employees have toward the new procedure
    D. what alterations in job descriptions will be necessitated by the new procedure

22. From the viewpoint of an office supervisor, the BEST of the following reasons for distributing the incoming mail *before* the beginning of the regular work day is that

    A. distribution can be handled quickly and most efficiently at that time
    B. distribution later in the day may be distracting to or interfere with other employees
    C. the employees who distribute the mail can then perform other tasks during the rest of the day
    D. office activities for the day based on the mail may then be started promptly

23. Suppose you are the head of a unit with ten staff members who are located in several different rooms. If you want to inform your staff of a *minor* change in procedure, the BEST and LEAST expensive way of doing so would usually be to

    A. send a mimeographed copy to each staff member
    B. call a special staff meeting and announce the change
    C. circulate a memo, having each staff member initial it
    D. have a clerk tell each member of the staff about the change

24. The numbered statements below relate to the stenographic skill of taking dictation. According to authorities on secretarial practices, which of these are GENERALLY recommended guides to development of efficient stenographic skills?
    A stenographer should

    I. date her notebook daily to facilitate locating certain notes at a later time
    II. make corrections of grammatical mistakes while her boss is dictating to her
    III. draw a line through the dictated matter in her notebook after she has transcribed it
    IV. write in longhand unfamiliar names and addresses dictated to her

    The CORRECT answer is:

    A. I, II, III
    B. II, III, IV
    C. I, III, IV
    D. All of the above

25. A bureau of a city agency is about to move to a new location.
    Of the following, the FIRST step that should be taken in order to provide a good layout for the office at the new location is to

A. decide the exact amount of space to be assigned to each unit of the bureau
B. decide whether to lay out a single large open office or one consisting of small partitioned units
C. ask each unit chief in the bureau to examine the new location and submit a request for the amount of space he needs
D. prepare a detailed plan of the dimensions of the floor space to be occupied by the bureau at the new location

KEY (CORRECT ANSWERS)

1. A
2. B
3. B
4. C
5. A

6. A
7. D
8. B
9. A
10. D

11. A
12. D
13. A
14. B
15. A

16. C
17. B
18. C
19. C
20. B

21. B
22. D
23. C
24. C
25. D

TEST 2

DIRECTIONS: Each question or incomplete statement is followed by several suggested answers or completions. Select the one that BEST answers the question or completes the statement. *PRINT THE LETTER OF THE CORRECT ANSWER IN THE SPACE AT THE RIGHT.*

1. Suppose you are the supervisor of the mailroom of a large agency where the mail received daily is opened by machine, sorted by hand for delivery and time-stamped. Letters and any enclosures are removed from envelopes and stapled together before distribution. One of your newest clerks asks you what should be done when a letter makes reference to an enclosure, but no enclosure is in the envelope.
   You should tell him that in this situation the BEST procedure is to

   A. make an entry of the sender's name and address in the "missing enclosures" file and forward the letter to its proper destination
   B. return the letter to its sender, attaching a request for the missing enclosure
   C. put the letter aside until a proper investigation may be made concerning the missing enclosure
   D. route the letter to the person for whom it is intended, noting the absence of the enclosure on the letter margin

2. The term "work flow," when used in connection with office management or the activities in an office, GENERALLY means the

   A. use of charts in the analysis of various office functions
   B. rate of speed at which work flows through a single section of an office
   C. step-by-step physical routing of work through its various procedures
   D. number of individual work units which can be produced by the average employee

3. Physical conditions can have a definite effect on the efficiency and morale of an office. Which of the following statements about physical conditions in an office is CORRECT?

   A. Hard, non-porous surfaces reflect more noise than linoleum on the top of a desk.
   B. Painting in tints of bright yellow is more appropriate for sunny, well-lit offices than for dark, poorly-lit offices.
   C. Plate glass is better than linoleum for the top of a desk.
   D. The central typing room needs less light than a conference room does.

4. In a certain filing system, documents are consecutively numbered as they are filed, a register is maintained of such consecutively numbered documents, and a record is kept of the number of each document removed from the files and its destination.
   This system will NOT help in

   A. finding the present whereabouts of a particular document
   B. proving the accuracy of the data recorded on a certain document
   C. indicating whether observed existing documents were ever filed
   D. locating a desired document without knowing what its contents are

5. In deciding the kind and number of records an agency should keep, the administrative staff must recognize that records are of value in office management PRIMARILY as

A. informational bases for agency activities
B. data for evaluating the effectiveness of the agency
C. raw material on which statistical analyses are to be based
D. evidence that the agency is carrying out its duties and responsibilities

6. Complaints are often made by the public about the city government's procedures. Although in most cases such procedures cannot be changed since various laws and regulations require them, it may still be possible to reduce the number of complaints. Which one of the following actions by personnel dealing with applicants for city services is LEAST likely to reduce complaints concerning city procedures?

    A. Treating all citizens alike and explaining to them that no exceptions to required procedures can be made
    B. Explaining briefly to the citizen why he should comply with regulations
    C. Being careful to avoid mistakes which may make additional interviews or correspondence necessary
    D. Keeping the citizen informed of the progress of his correspondence when immediate disposition cannot be made

7. In answering a complaint made by a member of the public that a certain essential procedure required by your agency is difficult to follow, it would be BEST for you to stress MOST

    A. that a change in the rules may be considered if enough complaints are received
    B. why the operation of a large agency sometimes proves a hardship in individual cases
    C. the necessity for the procedure
    D. the origin of the procedure

8. When talking to a citizen, it is BEST for an employee of government to

    A. use ordinary conversational phrases and a natural manner
    B. try to copy the pronunciation and level of education shown by the citizen
    C. try to speak in a very cultured manner and tone
    D. use technical terms to show his familiarity with his own work

9. Employees who service the public should maintain an attitude which is both sympathetic and objective.
An UNSYMPATHETIC and SUBJECTIVE attitude would be shown by a public employee who

    A. says "no" with a smile when a citizen's request must be denied
    B. listens attentively to a long complaint from a citizen about the government's "red tape"
    C. responds with sarcasm when a citizen asks a question which has an obvious answer
    D. suggests a definite solution to a citizen's problems

10. You are a supervisor in a city agency and are holding your first interview with a new employee.
In this interview, you should strive MAINLY to

A. show the new employee that you are an efficient and objective supervisor, with a completely impersonal attitude toward your subordinates
B. complete the entire orientation process including the giving of detailed job-duty instructions
C. make it clear to the employee that all your decisions are based on your many years of experience
D. lay the groundwork for a good employee-supervisor relationship by gaining the new employee's confidence

11. A senior clerk or senior typist may be required to help train a newly-appointed clerk. Which of the following is LEAST important for a newly-appointed clerk to know in order to perform his work efficiently? 11.____

    A. Acceptable ways of answering and recording telephone calls
    B. The number of files in the storage files unit
    C. The filing methods used by his unit
    D. Proper techniques for handling visitors

12. In your agency, you have the responsibility of processing clients who have appointments with agency representatives. On a particularly busy day, a client comes to your desk and insists that she must see the person handling her case although she has no appointment.
    Under the circumstances, your FIRST action should be to 12.____

    A. show her the full appointment schedule
    B. give her an appointment for another day
    C. ask her to explain the urgency
    D. tell her to return later in the day

13. Which of the following practices is BEST for a supervisor to use when assigning work to his staff? 13.____

    A. Give workers with seniority the most difficult jobs
    B. Assign all unimportant work to the slower workers
    C. Permit each employee to pick the job he prefers
    D. Make assignments based on the workers' abilities

14. In which of the following instances is a supervisor MOST justified in giving commands to people under his supervision? When 14.____

    A. they delay in following instructions which have been given to them clearly
    B. they become relaxed and slow about work, and he wants to speed up their production
    C. he must direct them in an emergency situation
    D. he is instructing them on jobs that are unfamiliar to them

15. Which of the following supervisory actions or attitudes is MOST likely to result in getting subordinates to try to do as much work as possible for a supervisor? He 15.____

    A. shows that his most important interest is in schedules and production goals
    B. consistently pressures his staff to get the work out
    C. never fails to let them know he is in charge
    D. considers their abilities and needs while requiring that production goals be met

16. Assume that a senior clerk has been explaining certain regulations to a new clerk under his supervision.
    The MOST efficient way for the senior clerk to make sure that the clerk has understood the explanation is to

    A. give him written materials on the regulations
    B. ask him if he has any further questions about the regulations
    C. ask him specific questions based on what has just been explained to him
    D. watch the way he handles a situation involving these regulations

17. One of your unit clerks has been assigned to work for a Mr. Jones in another office for several days. At the end of the first day, Mr. Jones, saying the clerk was not satisfactory, asks that she not be assigned to him again. This clerk is one of your most dependable workers, and no previous complaints about her work have come to you from any other outside assignments.
    To get to the root of this situation, your FIRST action should be to

    A. ask Mr. Jones to explain in what way her work was unsatisfactory
    B. ask the clerk what she did that Mr. Jones considered unsatisfactory
    C. check with supervisors for whom she previously worked to see if your own rating of her is in error
    D. tell Mr. Jones to pick the clerk he would prefer to have work for him the next time

18. A senior typist, still on probation, is instructed to type, as quickly as possible, one section of a draft of a long, complex report. Her part must be typed and readable before another part of the report can be written. Asked when she can have the report ready, she gives her supervisor an estimate of a day longer than she knows it will actually take. She then finishes the job a day sooner than the date given her supervisor.
    The judgment shown by a senior typist in giving an overestimate of time in a situation like this is, in general,

    A. *good,* because it prevents the supervisor from thinking she works slowly
    B. *good,* because it keeps unrealistic supervisors from expecting too much
    C. *bad,* because she should have used the time left to further check and proofread her work
    D. *bad,* because schedules and plans for other parts of the project may have been based on her false estimate

19. Suppose a new clerk, still on probation, is placed under your supervision and refuses to do a job you ask him to do.
    What is the FIRST thing you should do?

    A. Explain that you are the supervisor, and he must follow your instructions.
    B. Tell him he may be suspended if he refuses.
    C. Ask someone else to do the job, and rate him accordingly.
    D. Ask for his reason for objecting to the request.

20. As a supervisor of a small group of people, you have blamed worker A for something that you later find out was really done by worker B.
    The BEST thing for you to do now would be to

    A. say nothing to worker A, but criticize worker B for his mistake while worker A is near so that A will realize that you know who made the mistake
    B. speak to each worker separately, apologize to worker A for your mistake, and discuss worker B's mistake with him
    C. bring both workers together, apologize to worker A for your mistake, and discuss worker B's mistake with him
    D. say nothing new but be careful about mixing up worker A with worker B in the future

21. You have just learned one of your staff is grumbling that she thinks you are not pleased with her work. As far as you are concerned, this is not true at all. In fact, you have paid no particular attention to this worker lately because you have been very busy. You have just finished preparing an important report and "breaking in" a new clerk.
    Under the circumstances, the BEST thing to do is

    A. ignore her; after all, it is just a figment of her imagination
    B. discuss the matter with her now to try to find out and eliminate the cause of this problem
    C. tell her not to worry about it; you have not had time to think about her work
    D. make a note to meet with her at a later date in order to straighten out the situation

22. A most important job of a supervisor is to positively motivate employees to increase their work production. Which of the following LEAST indicates that a group of workers has been positively motivated?

    A. Their work output becomes constant and stable.
    B. Their cooperation at work becomes greater.
    C. They begin to show pride in the product of their work.
    D. They show increased interest in their work.

23. Which of the following traits would be LEAST important in considering a person for a merit increase?

    A. Punctuality
    B. Using initiative successfully
    C. High rate of production
    D. Resourcefulness

24. Of the following, the action LEAST likely to gain a supervisor the cooperation of his staff is for him to

    A. give each person consideration as an individual
    B. be as objective as possible when evaluating work performance
    C. rotate the least popular assignments
    D. expect subordinates to be equally competent

25. It has been said that, for the supervisor, nothing can beat the "face-to-face" communication of talking to one subordinate at a time.
    This method is, however, LEAST appropriate to use when the

    A. supervisor is explaining a change in general office procedure
    B. subject is of personal importance
    C. supervisor is conducting a yearly performance evaluation of all employees
    D. supervisor must talk to some of his employees concerning their poor attendance and punctuality

KEY (CORRECT ANSWERS)

1.	D	11.	B
2.	C	12.	C
3.	A	13.	D
4.	B	14.	C
5.	A	15.	D
6.	A	16.	C
7.	C	17.	A
8.	A	18.	D
9.	C	19.	D
10.	D	20.	B

21. B
22. A
23. A
24. D
25. A

TEST 3

DIRECTIONS: Each question or incomplete statement is followed by several suggested answers or completions. Select the one that BEST answers the question or completes the statement. *PRINT THE LETTER OF THE CORRECT ANSWER IN THE SPACE AT THE RIGHT.*

1. While you are on the telephone answering a question about your agency, a visitor comes to your desk and starts to ask you a question. There is no emergency or urgency in either situation, that of the phone call or that of answering the visitor's question.
   In this case, you should

   A. continue to answer the person on the telephone until you are finished and then tell the visitor you are sorry to have kept him waiting
   B. excuse yourself to the person on the telephone and tell the visitor that you will be with him as soon as you have finished on the phone
   C. explain to the person on the telephone that you have a visitor and must shorten the conversation
   D. continue to answer the person on the phone while looking up occasionally at the visitor to let him know that you know he is waiting

   1.____

2. While speaking on the telephone to someone who called, you are disconnected.
   The FIRST thing you should do is

   A. hang up, but try to keep your line free to receive the call back
   B. immediately get the dial tone and continually dial the person who called you until you reach him
   C. signal the switchboard operator and ask her to re-establish the connection
   D. dial "O" for Operator and explain that you were disconnected

   2.____

3. The type of speech used by an office worker in telephone conversation greatly affects the communication.
   Of the following, the BEST way to express your ideas when telephoning is with a vocabulary that consists MAINLY of

   A. formal, intellectual sounding words
   B. often used colloquial words
   C. technical, emphatic words
   D. simple, descriptive words

   3.____

4. Suppose a clerk under your supervision has taken a personal phone call and is at the same time needed to answer a question regarding an assignment being handled by another member of your office. He appears confused as to what he should do. How should you instruct him later as to how to handle a similar situation?
   You should tell him to

   A. tell the caller to hold on while he answers the question
   B. tell the caller to call back a little later
   C. return the call during an assigned break
   D. finish the conversation quickly and answer the question

   4.____

5. You are asked to place a telephone call by your supervisor. When you place the call, you receive what appears to be a wrong number.
   Of the following, you should FIRST

   A. check the number with your supervisor to see if the number he gave you is correct
   B. ask the person on the other end what his number is and who he is
   C. check with the person on the other end to see if the number you dialed is the number you received
   D. apologize to the person on the other end for disturbing him and hang up

6. When you select someone to serve as supervisor of your unit during your absence on vacation and at other times, it would generally be BEST to choose the employee who is

   A. able to move the work along smoothly, without friction
   B. on staff longest
   C. liked best by the rest of the staff
   D. able to perform the work of each employee to be supervised

7. Successful supervision of handicapped persons employed in a department depends MOST on providing them with a work place and work climate

   A. which is safe and accident-free
   B. that requires close and direct supervision by others
   C. that requires the performance of routine, repetitive tasks under a minimum of pressure
   D. where they will be accepted by the other employees

8. Studies have indicated that when employees feel that their work is aimless and unchallenging, the allocation or payment of more money for this type of work is likely to

   A. contribute little to increased production
   B. bring more status to this work
   C. increase employees' feelings of security
   D. give employees greater motivation

9. An employee's performance has fallen below established minimum standards of quantity and quality.
   The threat of monetary or other disciplinary action as a device for improving this employee's performance would probably be acceptable and MOST effective

   A. only if applied as soon as the performance fell below standard
   B. only after more constructive techniques have failed
   C. at any time provided the employee understands that the punishment will be carried out
   D. at no time

10. A supervisor must, on short notice, ask his staff to work overtime.
    Of the following, a technique that is MOST likely to win their willing cooperation would be to

    A. explain that occasional overtime is part of the job requirement
    B. explain that they will be doing him a personal favor which he will appreciate very much

    C. explain why the overtime is necessary
    D. promise them that they can take the extra time off in the near future

11. On checking a completed work assignment of an employee, the supervisor finds that the work was not done correctly because the employee had not understood his instructions. Of the following, the BEST way to prevent repetition of this situation next time is for the supervisor to

    A. ask the employee whether he fully understood the instructions and tell him to ask questions in the future whenever anything is unclear
    B. ask the employee to repeat the instructions given and test his understanding with several key questions
    C. give the instructions a second time, emphasizing the more complicated aspects of the job
    D. give work instructions in writing

12. If, as a supervisor, you find yourself pressured for time to handle all of your job responsibilities, the one of the following tasks which it would be MOST appropriate for you to delegate to a subordinate is

    A. attending a staff conference of unit supervisors to discuss the implementation of a new departmental policy
    B. making staff work assignments
    C. interviewing a new employee
    D. checking work of certain employees for accuracy

13. Suppose you are unavoidably late for work one morning. When you arrive at 10 o'clock, you find there are several matters demanding your attention.
    Which one of the following matters should you handle LAST?

    A. A visitor who had a 9:30 appointment with you has been waiting to see you since 9 o'clock.
    B. An employee on an assignment which should have been completed that morning is absent, and the work will have to be reassigned.
    C. Several letters which you dictated at the end of the previous day have been typed and are on your desk for signature and mailing.
    D. Your superior called asking you to get certain information for him when you come in and to call him back.

14. Suppose that you have assigned a typist to type a report containing considerable statistical and tabular material and have given her specific instructions as to how this material is to be laid out on each page. When she returns the completed report, you find that it was not prepared according to your instructions, but you may possibly be able to use it the way it was typed. When you question her, she states that she thought her layout was better but you were unavailable for consultation when she began the work.
    Of the following, the BEST action for you to take is to

    A. criticize her for not doing the work according to your instructions
    B. have her retype the report
    C. praise her for her work but tell her she should have waited until she could consult you
    D. praise her for using initiative

15. Of the following, the MOST effective way for a supervisor to correct poor work habits of an employee which result in low and poor quality output is to give the employee   15.____

    A. additional training
    B. less demanding assignments until his work improves
    C. continuous supervision
    D. more severe criticism

16. Of the following, the BEST way for a supervisor to teach an employee how to do a new and somewhat complicated job is to   16.____

    A. assign him to observe another employee who is already skilled in this work and instruct him to consult this employee if he has any questions
    B. explain to him how to do it, then demonstrate how it is done, then observe and correct the employee as he does it, then follow up
    C. give him a written, detailed, step-by-step explanation of how to do the job and instruct him to ask questions if anything is unclear when he does the work
    D. teach him the easiest part of the job first, then the other parts one at a time, in order of their difficulty, as the employee masters the easier parts

17. After an employee has completed telling his supervisor about a grievance against a co-worker, the supervisor tells the employee that he will take action to remove the cause of the grievance.
    The action of the supervisor was   17.____

    A. *good,* because ill feeling between subordinates interferes with proper performance
    B. *poor,* because the supervisor should give both employees time to "cool off"
    C. *good,* because grievances that appear petty to the supervisor are important to subordinates
    D. *poor,* because the supervisor should tell the employee that he will investigate the matter before he comes to any conclusion

18. During work on an important project, one employee in a secretarial pool turns in several pages of typed copy, one page of which contains several errors.
    Of these four comments which her supervisor might possibly make, which one would be MOST constructive?   18.____

    A. "You did such a poor job on this; I will have to have it done over."
    B. "You will have to do better, more consistently than this, if you want to be in charge of a secretarial pool yourself someday."
    C. "How come you made so many mistakes here? Your other pages were all right."
    D. "If my boss saw this, he would be very displeased with you."

19. A supervisor has general supervision over a large, complex project with many employees. The work is subdivided among small units of employees, each with a senior clerk or senior stenographer in charge. At a staff meeting, after all work assignments have been made, the supervisor tells all the employees that they are to take orders only from their immediate supervisor and instructs them to let him know if anyone else tries to give them orders.
    This instruction by the supervising clerk is   19.____

A. *good,* because it may prevent the issuance of orders by unauthorized persons, which would interfere with the accomplishment of the assignment
B. *poor,* because employees should be instructed to take up such problems with their immediate supervisor
C. *good,* because orders issued by immediate supervisors would be precise and directly related to the tasks of the assignments while those issued by others would not be
D. *poor,* because it places upon all employees a responsibility which should not normally be theirs

20. A supervisor who is to direct a team of senior clerks and clerks in a complex project, calls them together beforehand to inform them of the tasks each employee will perform on this job.
Of the following, the CHIEF value of this action by the supervisor is that each member of this team will be able to

    A. work independently in the absence of the supervisor
    B. understand what he will do and how this will fit into the total picture
    C. share in the process of decision-making as an equal participant
    D. judge how well the plans for this assignment have been made

21. A supervisor who has both younger and older employees under his supervision may sometimes find that employee absenteeism seriously interferes with accomplishment of goals.
Studies of such employee absenteeism have shown that the absences of employees

    A. under 35 years of age are usually unexpected and the absences of employees over 45 years of age are usually unnecessary
    B. of all age groups show the same characteristics as to length of absence
    C. under 35 years of age are for frequent, short periods while the absences of employees over 45 years of age are less frequent but of longer duration
    D. under 35 years of age are for periods of long duration and the absences of employees over 45 years of age are for periods of short duration

22. Suppose you have a long-standing procedure for getting a certain job done by your subordinates that is apparently a good one. Changes in some steps of the procedure are made from time to time to handle special problems that come up.
For you to review this procedure periodically is desirable MAINLY because

    A. the system is working well
    B. checking routines periodically is a supervisor's chief responsibility
    C. subordinates may be confused as to how the procedure operates as a result of the changes made
    D. it is necessary to determine whether the procedure has become outdated or is in need of improvement

23. Suppose that a stranger enters the office you are in charge of and asks for the address and telephone number of one of your employees.
Of the following, it would be BEST for you to

    A. find out why he needs the information and release it if his reason is a good one
    B. explain that you are not permitted to release such information to unauthorized persons

C. give him the information but tell him it must be kept confidential
D. ask him to leave the office immediately

24. A member of the public approaches an employee who is at work at his desk. The employee cannot interrupt his work in order to take care of this person.
Of the following, the BEST and MOST courteous way of handling this situation is for the employee to

    A. avoid looking up from his work until he is finished with what he is doing
    B. tell this person that he will not be able to take care of him for quite a while
    C. refer the individual to another employee who can take care of him right away
    D. chat with the individual while he continues with his work

25. You answer a phone call from a citizen who urgently needs certain information you do not have, but you think you know who may have it. He is angry because he has already been switched to two different offices.
Of the following, it would be BEST for you to

    A. give him the phone number of the person you think may have the information he wants, but explain you are not sure
    B. tell him you regret you cannot help him because you are not sure who can give him the information
    C. advise him that the best way he can be sure of getting the information he wants is to write a letter to the agency
    D. get the phone number where he can be reached and tell him you will try to get the information he wants and will call him back later

KEY (CORRECT ANSWERS)

1.	B	11.	B
2.	A	12.	D
3.	D	13.	C
4.	C	14.	A
5.	C	15.	A
6.	A	16.	B
7.	D	17.	D
8.	A	18.	C
9.	B	19.	B
10.	C	20.	B

21. C
22. D
23. B
24. C
25. D

EXAMINATION SECTION
TEST 1

DIRECTIONS: Each question or incomplete statement is followed by several suggested answers or completions. Select the one that BEST answers the question or completes the statement. *PRINT THE LETTER OF THE CORRECT ANSWER IN THE SPACE AT THE RIGHT.*

1. From time to time, your subordinates are assigned to other units to do reception work and other duties. You receive a note from Mr. Jones, the head of one of these other units, stating that the work of Miss Smith, one of your subordinates, was unsatisfactory when she worked for him, and asking you not to assign her to him again. Although Miss Smith has worked in your unit for a long time, this is the first time that anyone has complained about her work.
   The one of the following actions that you should take FIRST in this situation is to ask
   A. the heads of the other units for whom Miss Smith has worked whether or not her work has been satisfactory
   B. Mr. Jones in what way Miss Smith's work has been unsatisfactory
   C. Miss Smith to explain in what way her work for Mr. Jones was unsatisfactory
   D. Mr. Jones which of your subordinates he would prefer to have assigned to him

1._____

2. Suppose that you are the supervisor of a small unit in a city agency. You have given one of your subordinates, Mr. Smith, an assignment which must be completed by the end of the day. Because he is unfamiliar with the assignment, Mr. Smith will be unable to complete it on time. Your other subordinates are too busy to help Mr. Smith, but you have the time to help him complete the assignment.
   For you to help Mr. Smith complete the assignment would be
   A. *desirable*; because a supervisor is expected to be familiar with his subordinates' work
   B. *undesirable*; because Mr. Smith will come to depend on you to help him do his work
   C. *desirable*; because Mr. Smith is likely to appreciate your help and give you his cooperation when you need it
   D. *undesirable*; because a supervisor should not perform the same type of work as his subordinates do

2._____

3. For a supervisor to listen to the personal problems which his subordinates bring to him is GENERALLY
   A. *desirable*; it is likely that the supervisor has broader experience in solving personal problems than do his subordinates
   B. *undesirable*; the supervisor may be unable to solve such problems

3._____

C. *desirable*; the supervisor can better understand his subordinates' behavior on the job
D. *undesirable*; permitting a subordinate to talk about his personal problems may only make them seem worse

4. A generally accepted concept of management is that the authority given to a person should be commensurate with his
    A. responsibility
    B. ability
    C. seniority
    D. dependability

5. It has been said that the best supervisor is the one who gives the fewest orders. The one of the following supervisor practices that would be MOT likely to increase the number of orders that a supervisor must give to get out the work is to
    A. set general goals for his subordinates and give them the authority for reaching the goals
    B. train subordinates to make decisions for themselves
    C. establish routines for his subordinates' jobs
    D. introduce frequent changes in the work methods his subordinates are using

6. The one of the following supervisory practices that would be MOST likely to give subordinates a feeling of satisfaction in their work is to
    A. establish work goals that take a long time to achieve
    B. show the subordinates how their work goals are related to the goals of the agency
    C. set work goals higher than the subordinates can achieve
    D. refrain from telling the subordinates that they are failing to meet their work goals

7. You are about to design a system for measuring the quantity of work produced by your subordinates.
    The one of the following which is the FIRST step that you should take in designing this system is to
    A. establish the units of work measurement to be used in the system
    B. determine the actual advantages and disadvantages of the system
    C. determine the abilities of each of your subordinates
    D. ascertain the types of work done in the unit

8. One of your subordinates tells you that he is dissatisfied with his work assignment and that he wishes to discuss the matter with you. The employee is obviously very angry and upset.
    Of the following, the course of action that you should take FIRST in this situation is to
    A. postpone discussion of the employee's complaint, explaining to him that the matter can be settled more satisfactorily if it is discussed calmly
    B. have the employee describe his complaint, correcting him whenever he makes what seems to be an erroneous charge against you

C. permit the employee to present his complaint in full, withholding your comments until he has finished describing his complaint
D. promise the employee that you will review all the work assignments in the unit to determine whether or not any changes should be made

9. Assume that you are the supervisor of a unit in a city agency. One of your subordinates has violated an important rule of the agency. For such a violation, you are required to impose discipline in the form of a reprimand given in private.
Of the following, the MOST important reason for disciplining the employee for violating the rule is to
   A. obtain his compliance with the rule
   B. punish him for his action in an impartial manner
   C. establish your authority to administer discipline
   D. impress upon all the employees in the unit the need for observing the rule

10. You are the newly appointed supervisor of a small unit in a city agency. One of your subordinates, Mr. Smith, a competent employee, has resented your appointment as his supervisor and has not been as cooperative toward you as you have wanted him to be. One day, Mr. Smith fails to observe an important rule of the agency. You are required to reprimand any employee who fails to observe the rule.
The one of the following courses of action you should take in this situation is to
   A. attempt to overcome Mr. Smith's resentment by explaining to him that although you should reprimand him, you will not do so
   B. reprimand Mr. Smith after pointing out to him that he failed to observe the rule
   C. tell Mr. Smith that if he becomes more cooperative, you will overlook his failure to observe the rule
   D. tell Mr. Smith that although you did not originate the rule, nevertheless you are required to reprimand him

11. Suppose that a clerk who has injured himself on the job because of his carelessness informs his supervisor of the accident. The supervisor has been newly appointed to his job and is anxious to keep accidents at a minimum. The action taken by the supervisor is to criticize the subordinate for his carelessness and to tell him that he is holding him responsible for the accident.
Of the following, it would be MOST reasonable to conclude that, as a result of the supervisor's action, his subordinates may
   A. tend to withhold information from him about future accidents
   B. be critical of him, in turn, if he himself is injured on the job
   C. expect him to supervise them more closely in the future
   D. attempt to correct hazardous job conditions without his knowledge

12. The one of the following which is GENERALLY the basic reason for using standard procedures in an agency is to
   A. provide sequences of steps for handling recurring activities
   B. facilitate periodic review of standard practices

C. train new employees in the agency's policies and objectives
D. serve as a basis for formulating agency policies

13. Assume that the operations of a certain unit in an agency enable the supervisor to allow each of his subordinates wide discretion in selecting the kind and amount of work he chooses to do. However, in evaluating the work of his subordinates, the supervisor places more emphasis on some area of work than on others. Factors such as number of applications processed and number of letters written are given great weight in evaluation, while factors such as number of papers filed and number of forms checked are given little weight. Hence, a subordinate who processes a large number of applications would receive a high evaluation even if he checked very few forms.
The supervisor's method of evaluation would MOST likely result in a(n)
    A. increase in the amount of time spent on processing each application
    B. backlog of papers waiting to be filed
    C. improvement in the quality of letters written
    D. decline in output in all areas of work

13.____

14. Some management authorities propose that work assignments be made by assigning a varied set of tasks to a group of employees and then allowing the group to decide for itself how to organize the work to be done. This method of assigning work is called *job enlargement*.
The one of the following which is considered to be the CHIEF advantage of job enlargement is that it
    A. encourages employees to specialize in the work they are assigned to do
    B. reduces the amount of control that employees have over their work
    C. increases the employees' job satisfaction
    D. reduces the number of skills that each employee is required to learn

14.____

15. In conducting a meeting to pass along information to his subordinates, a supervisor may talk to his subordinates without giving them the opportunity to interrupt him. This method is called one-way communication. On the other hand, the supervisor may talk to his subordinates and give them the opportunity to ask questions or make comments while he is speaking. This method is called two-way communication.
It would be MORE desirable for the supervisor to use two-way communication rather than one-way communication at a meeting when his primary purpose is to
    A. avoid, during the meeting, open criticism of any mistakes he may make
    B. conduct the meeting in an orderly fashion
    C. pass along information quickly
    D. transmit information which must be clearly understood

15.____

16. Assume that you are the leader of a training conference on supervisory techniques and problems. One of the participants in the conference proposes what you consider to be an unsatisfactory technique for handling the problem under discussion.

16.____

The one of the following courses of action which you should take in this situation is to
- A. explain to the participants why the proposed technique is unsatisfactory
- B. stimulate the other participants to discuss the appropriateness of the proposed technique
- C. proceed immediately to another problem without discussing the proposed technique
- D. end further discussion of the problem but explain to the participant in private, after the conference is over, why he proposed technique is unsatisfactory

17. In measuring the work of his subordinates, the supervisor of a unit performing routine filing began by observing his subordinates at work. If a subordinate seemed to be busy, then the supervisor concluded that the subordinate was producing a great deal of work. On the other hand, the supervisor concluded that a subordinate was not producing much work if he did not seem to be busy. The supervisor's work measurement method was faulted CHIEFLY because
    - A. it did not use a standard against which a subordinate's work could be measured
    - B. the type of work performed by his subordinates did not lend itself to accurate measurement
    - C. his subordinates may not have worked at their normal rates if they were aware that their work was being observed
    - D. the supervisor may not have observed a subordinate's work for a long enough period of time

17.____

18. Assume that a system of statistical reports designed to provide information about employee work performance is put into effect in a unit of a city agency. There is some evidence that the employees of this unit are working below their capacities. The information obtained from the system is to be used by management to improve employee work and performance and to evaluate such performance. The employees whose work is to be recorded by the reports resent them. Nevertheless, the employees' work performance improves substantially after the reporting system is put into effect, and before management has put the information to use.
The one of the following which is the MOST accurate conclusion to be drawn from this situation is that
    - A. a statistical reporting system may fail to provide the information it is designed to provide
    - B. low employee morale may have been the cause of the employees' former level of work performance
    - C. a statistical reporting system designed only to provide information about problems may also help to solve the problems
    - D. willing employee cooperation is essential to the success of a system of statistical reports

18.____

19. In setting the work standard for a certain task, a unit supervisor took the total output of all the employees in the unit and divided it by the number of employees. He thus established the average output as the work standard for the task.
    The method that the supervisor used to establish the work standard is GENERALLY considered to be
    A. *proper,* since the method takes into account the output of the outstanding, as well as of the less productive, employees
    B. *improper,* since the average output may not be what could reasonably be expected of a competent, satisfactory employee
    C. *proper,* since the standard is based on the actual output of the employees who are to be evaluated
    D. *improper,* since all the employees in the unit may be successful in meeting the work standard

20. There are disadvantages as well as advantages in using statistical controls to measure specific aspects of subordinates' jobs.
    The one of the following which can LEAST be considered to be an advantage of statistical controls to a supervisor is that such controls may
    A. reduce the need for close, detailed supervision
    B. give the supervisor information that he needs for making decisions
    C. stimulate subordinates whose work is measured by statistical controls to improve their performance
    D. encourage subordinates to emphasize aspects being measured rather than their jobs as a whole

21. Mr. Stone, who has been recently placed in charge of a clerical unit staffed with ten employees, plans to institute several radical changes in the procedures of his unit.
    Of the following actions he may take before adopting any of the revisions, the MOST desirable one is for Mr. Stone to
    A. distribute to each staff member a memorandum describing the revised procedures and requesting the staff's cooperation in giving the revised procedures a fair trial
    B. issue to each staff member a memorandum describing the proposed changes and inviting him to submit his written criticism of these proposed changes
    C. issue to each staff member a memorandum describing the proposed changes and notifying him of the time and date of a staff conference to be held on the merits
    D. of the proposed changes discuss the proposed changes with each staff member independently and obtain his opinion of the proposed changes

22. An assignment completed by Frank King is returned to him by his unit supervisor for certain changes. Frank King objects to making these changes.
    Of the following, the MOST appropriate action for the unit supervisor to take FIRST is to
    A. permit Frank King to present his arguments against making these changes

7 (#1)

  B. inform Frank King that he is free to take the matter up with a higher authority
  C. reprimand Frank King for objecting and assign another employee to make these changes
  D. state briefly that his decision is final and indicate by his manner that further discussion would be useless

23. Of the following, it is LEAST essential for a supervisor, in assigning work to a subordinate, to issue written instructions when the
  A. supervisor will be on hand to check the work
  B. instructions are to be passed on to other employees
  C. assignment involves many details
  D. subordinate is to be held strictly accountable for the work performed

23.____

24. Assume that you have been placed in charge of a unit where the quality of the work performed is poor. You plan to discuss the matter of improving the quality of the wok at a staff meeting of the unit.
Of the following courses of action which you might take at this meeting, the BEST one is to
  A. describe a few cases of exceptionally poor work performance; then have the employees performing this work explain why their work was done poorly
  B. inform the staff that you will be criticized by your own superior if the quality of the unit's work does not improve; then discuss, in general terms, the problem of improving the quality of the work
  C. discuss the problem of improving the quality of the unit's work; then call upon each employee by name for his suggestions for improving the work he performs
  D. present the problem to the staff; then indicate and discuss specific methods for improving the quality of the work

24.____

25. Suppose that certain office responsibilities require you to be frequently absent from the unit you supervise. You have, therefore, decided to designate one of your staff members to act as unit head in your absence.
Of the following factors, the one which is MOST important in selecting the employee best fitted for this assignment is his
  A. manner and personal appearance
  B. estimated ability to perform work of a supervisory nature
  C. ability to perform his present duties
  D. relative seniority in the service

25.____

KEY (CORRECT ANSWERS)

1.	B	11.	A
2.	C	12.	A
3.	C	13.	B
4.	A	14.	C
5.	D	15.	D
6.	B	16.	B
7.	D	17.	A
8.	C	18.	C
9.	A	19.	B
10.	B	20.	D

21. C
22. A
23. A
24. D
25. B

TEST 2

DIRECTIONS: Each question or incomplete statement is followed by several suggested answers or completions. Select the one that BEST answers the question or completes the statement. *PRINT THE LETTER OF THE CORRECT ANSWER IN THE SPACE AT THE RIGHT.*

1. Assume that your supervisor has placed you in complete charge of an important project and that several clerks have been assigned to assist you. You have been given authority to establish any new procedures or revise existing procedures in order to complete the project as soon as possible. Just before you begin work on the project, one of the clerks suggests a change in the procedure which you realize at once would result in completion of the project in about half the time you expected to spend on it.
   Of the following, the MOST effective course of action for you to take is to
   A. adopt the suggestion immediately to expedite the completion of the project
   B. discuss the suggestion with your superior to obtain his consent to the change
   C. point out to the clerk that an adequate procedure has already been established, but that his suggestion may be used in future projects of this type
   D. encourage the other clerks to make further suggestions

    1.____

2. A supervisor of a unit may safely delegate certain of his functions to his subordinates.
   Of the following, the function which can MOST safely be delegated is the
   A. settlement of employee grievances
   B. planning and scheduling of the production of the unit
   C. improvement of production methods of the unit
   D. maintenance of records of the work output of the unit

    2.____

3. Some organizations now question the effectiveness of extreme job specialization. It is felt that in some instances it may be more advantageous to enlarge the scope of individual jobs, thus providing the employee with a greater variety of tasks.
   Of the following, the one which is LEAST likely to be a result of enlarging the scope of jobs is a(n)
   A. increase in the employee's job responsibilities
   B. decrease in the number of job titles in the organization
   C. increase in the number of tasks performed by an employee
   D. decrease in employee flexibility

    3.____

4. A manual that is essentially designed to present detailed procedures and policies is not necessarily a good training medium, nor is a manual designed for high-level administrators likely to be satisfactory for use at lower levels.
   The MOST valid implication of this quotation is that
   A. a manual, to be effective, should be flexible enough to apply to any working level in an organization

    4.____

79

B. the uses to which a manual will be put and the people who will use it should be carefully determined before it is prepared
C. the more detailed procedures a manual contains, the more effective it will be for the use of administrators
D. the degree of difficulty encountered in the preparation of a manual varies with the purpose for which it is designed and the people for whom it is written

5. In assigning a complicated task to a group of subordinates, Mr. Jones, a unit supervisor, neither indicates the specific steps to be followed in performing the assignment nor designates the subordinate to be responsible for seeing that the task is done on time.
This supervisor's method of assigning the task is MOST likely to result in
    A. the loss of skills previously acquired by his subordinates
    B. assumption of authority by the most capable subordinates
    C. friction and misunderstanding among subordinates with consequent delays in work
    D. greater individual effort and self-reliance on the part of his subordinates

6. Assume that the head of your agency has appointed you to a committee that has been assigned the task of reviewing the clerical procedures used in a large bureau of the agency and of recommending appropriate changes in the procedures where necessary.
Of the following, the FIRST step that should be taken by the committee in carrying out its assignment is to
    A. survey the most efficient procedures used in comparable agencies
    B. study the organization of the bureau and the work it is required to do
    C. evaluate the possible effects of proposed revisions in the procedures
    D. determine the effectiveness of existing procedures

7. A recently developed practice in administration favors reducing the number of levels of authority in an organization, increasing the number of subordinates reporting to a superior, and also increasing the authority delegated to the subordinates.
This practice would MOST likely result in a(n)
    A. increase in the span of control exercised by superiors
    B. increase in detailed information that flows to a superior from each subordinate
    C. decrease in the responsibility exercised by the subordinates
    D. decrease in the number of functions performed by the subordinates

8. As an organization grows larger, the amount of personal contact between the top administrative officials and the rank and file employees diminishes. Consequently, management comes to rely more heavily upon written reports and records for securing information and exercising control.
The MOST valid implication of this quotation is that, as an organization grows larger,
    A. evaluation of the work of rank and file employees becomes more objective because of greater reliance upon written reports and records

B. relations between first-line supervisors and their subordinates grow more impersonal
C. top administrative officials depend upon less direct methods for controlling the work of their subordinates
D. it becomes more difficult for top administrative officials to maintain high morale among rank and file employees

9. A supervisor whose unit has a good production record is usually found to be more occupied with the functions associated with leadership than with the performance of the same functions as his subordinates.
The MOST valid implication of this quotation is that
   A. a supervisor whose unit has a good production record usually is not as competent in performing routine tasks as are his subordinates
   B. ability to lead and competence in performing the day-to-day tasks of his subordinates are the requirements of a successful supervisor
   C. a supervisor who spends more time on planning and organizing the work of his unit than on performing the routine tasks of his subordinates will find that a his unit's production record will be good
   D. a supervisor whose unit has a good production record usually places less emphasis on performing the day-to-day tasks of his subordinates than on planning the work of his unit

10. To delegate work is one of the main functions of the supervisor. In delegating work, the supervisor should remember that even though an assignment is delegated to a subordinate, the supervisor ultimately is responsible for seeing that the work is done.
The MOST valid implication of this quotation for a supervisor is that he should
   A. delegate as few difficult tasks as possible so as to minimize the consequences of inadequate performance by his subordinates
   B. delegate to his subordinates those tasks which he considers difficult or time-consuming
   C. check the progress of delegated assignments periodically to make certain that the work is being done properly
   D. assign work to a subordinate without holding him directly accountable for carrying it out

11. A supervisor should select and develop an understudy to take charge of the unit in the supervisor's absence and to assist the supervisor whenever necessary.
Of the following, the technique that would be LEAST effective in developing an understudy is for the supervisor to
   A. permit him to exercise complete supervision over certain parts of the work
   B. assign him to work in which there is little likelihood of his making mistakes, so as to increase his self-confidence
   C. accustom him to making reports on the progress of work he is supervising
   D. give him responsibility gradually so that he will have time to absorb each new responsibility

12. A procedure manual of an agency is potentially more usable than are files of individual messages or bulletins, but usability and usefulness are not routine by-products of the manual form.
    The MOST valid implication of this is that
    A. the purpose of a manual should not be confined to an explanation of routine procedures
    B. a manual may prove to be unsuitable for some of its anticipated uses
    C. individual messages or bulletins are more likely to be of use than are manuals
    D. a manual suffers from certain limitations that are not found in individual messages or bulletins

13. As the supervisor of a unit in an agency, you have just been instructed to put into effect a new procedure which you know will be disliked by your subordinates.
    Of the following, the MOST important reason for calling a meeting of your staff before putting the new procedure into effect is to
    A. help you to determine which workers will be reluctant to cooperate in carrying out the new procedure
    B. allow you to announce that the new procedure must be put into effect despite any objections which might be raised
    C. enable you to explain that you don't approve of the new procedure and to give the reasons why it must nevertheless be put into effect
    D. permit you to discuss the purpose of the new procedure and to present the reasons for its adoption

14. Assume that you are a training conference leader and that you have just begun a series of conferences on supervisory techniques for new supervisors. Each conference is scheduled to last for three hours. A thorough discussion of all the material planned for the first session, which you had estimated would last until 4 P.M., is completed by 3:30 P.M.
    For you to summarize the points that have been made and close the meeting would be
    A. *advisable*; the participants will lose interest in the conference if it is permitted to continue merely to occupy the remaining time
    B. *inadvisable*; the participants should be asked if there are any other topics that they would like to discuss
    C. *advisable*; the participants in a training conference should not be kept from their regular work for long periods of time
    D. *inadvisable*; material scheduled for discussion at future sessions should be used for the remainder of this session

15. In any agency, the top administrative officials are concerned largely with the work of overall creative planning with respect to the anticipated progress of the agency. The first-line supervisors, on the other hand, are concerned largely with the control of current action for the execution of current jobs.
    On the basis of this quotation, a first-line supervisor would be CHIEFLY responsible for

A. increasing or decreasing the responsibilities of his unit to reflect changes in the policies of the agency
B. modifying the work assignments of his present staff to handle a seasonal variation in the activities of the unit
C. revising the procedure that is used for transmitting instructions from the head of the agency to the unit heads
D. raising and lowering the production goals of his unit as often as necessary to adjust them to the abilities of his subordinates

16. The control of clerical work in an agency appears impossible if the clerical work is regarded merely as a series of duties unrelated to the functions of the agency. However, this control becomes feasible when it is realized that clerical work links and coordinates the functions of the agency.
On the basis of this quotation, the MOST accurate of the following statements is that the
    A. complexity of clerical work may not be fully understood by those assigned to control it
    B. clerical work can be readily controlled if it is coordinated by other work of the agency
    C. number of clerical tasks may be reduced by regarding coordination as the function of clerical work
    D. purposes of clerical work must be understood to make possible its proper control

17. Assume that as supervisor of a unit you are to prepare a vacation schedule for the employees in your unit.
Of the following, the factor which is LEAST important for you to consider in setting up this schedule is
    A. the vacation preferences of each employee in the unit
    B. the anticipated workload in the unit during the vacation period
    C. how well each employee has performed his work
    D. how essential a specific employee's services will be during the vacation period

18. In order to promote efficiency and economy in an agency, it is advisable for the management systematize and standardize procedures and relationships insofar as this can be done; however, excessive routinizing which does not permit individual contributions or achievements should be avoided.
On the basis of this quotation, it is MOST accurate to state that
    A. systematized procedures should be designed mainly to encourage individual achievements
    B. standardized procedures should allow for individual accomplishments
    C. systematization of procedures may not be possible in organizations which have a large variety of functions
    D. individual employees of an organization must fully accept standardized procedures if the procedures are to be effective

19. Trained employees work most efficiently and with a minimum expenditure of time and energy. Suitable equipment and definite, well-developed procedures are effective only when employees know how to use the equipment and procedures.
    This quotation means MOST NEARLY that
    A. employees can be trained most efficiently when suitable equipment and definite procedures are used
    B. training of employees is a costly but worthwhile investment
    C. suitable equipment and definite procedures are of greatest value when employees have been properly traced to use them
    D. the cost of suitable equipment and definite procedures is negligible when the saving in time and energy that they bring is considered

20. Assume that your supervisor has asked you to present to him comprehensive, periodic reports on the progress that your unit is making in meeting its work goals.
    For you to give your superior oral reports rather than written ones is
    A. *desirable*; it will be easier for him to transmit your oral reports to his superiors
    B. *undesirable*; the oral reports will provide no permanent record to which he may refer
    C. *undesirable*; there will be less opportunity for you to discuss the oral reports with him than the written ones
    D. *desirable*; the oral reports will require little time and effort to prepare

21. Assume that an employee under your supervision complains to you that your evaluation of his work is too low.
    The MOST appropriate action for you to take FIRST is to
    A. explain how you arrived at the evaluation of his work
    B. encourage him to improve the quality of his work by pointing out specifically how he can do so
    C. suggest that he appeal to an impartial higher authority if he disagrees with your evaluation
    D. point out to him specific instances in which his work has been unsatisfactory

22. The nature of the experience and education that are made a prerequisite to employment determines in large degree the training job to be done after employment begins.
    On the basis of this quotation, it is MOST accurate to state that
    A. the more comprehensive the experience and education required for employment, the more extensive the training that is usually given after appointment
    B. the training that is given to employees depends upon the experience and education required of them before appointment
    C. employees who possess the experience and education required for employment should need little additional training after appointment
    D. the nature of the work that employees are expected to perform determines the training that they will need

23. Assume that you are preparing a report evaluating the work of a clerk who was transferred to your unit from another unit in the agency about a year ago.
Of the following, the method that would probably be MOST helpful to you in making this evaluation is to
   A. consult the evaluations this employee received from his former supervisors
   B. observe this employee at his work for a week shortly before you prepare the report
   C. examine the employee's production records and compare them with the standards set for the position
   D. obtain tactfully from his fellow employees their frank opinions of his work

23._____

24. Of the following, the CHIEF value of a flow of work chart to the management of an organization is its usefulness in
   A. locating the causes of delay in carrying out an operation
   B. training new employees in the performance of their duties
   C. determining the effectiveness of the employees in the organization
   D. determining the accuracy of its organization chart

24._____

25. Assume that a procedure for handling certain office forms has just been extensively revised. As supervisor of a small unit, you are to instruct your subordinates in the use of the new procedure, which is rather complicated.
Of the following, it would be LEAST helpful to your subordinates for you to
   A. compare the revised procedure with the one it has replaced
   B. state that you believe the revised procedure to be better than the one it has replaced
   C. tell them that they will probably find it difficult to learn the new procedure
   D. give only a general outline of the revised procedure at first and then follow with more detailed instructions

25._____

KEY (CORRECT ANSWERS)

1.	A	11.	B
2.	D	12.	B
3.	D	13.	D
4.	B	14.	A
5.	C	15.	B
6.	B	16.	B
7.	A	17.	C
8.	C	18.	B
9.	D	19.	C
10.	C	20.	B

21. A
22. B
23. C
24. A
25. C

TEST 3

DIRECTIONS: Each question or incomplete statement is followed by several suggested answers or completions. Select the one that BEST answers the question or completes the statement. *PRINT THE LETTER OF THE CORRECT ANSWER IN THE SPACE AT THE RIGHT.*

1. A methods improvement program might be called a war against habit.
   The MOST accurate implication of this statement is that
   A. routine handling of routine office assignments should be discouraged
   B. standardization of office procedures may encourage employees to form inefficient work habits
   C. employees tend to continue the use of existing procedures, even when such procedures are inefficient
   D. procedures should be changed consistently to prevent them from becoming habits

   1.____

2. An office supervisor may give either a written or an oral order to his subordinates when making an assignment.
   Of the following, it would be MOST appropriate for a supervisor to issue an order in writing when
   A. a large number of two-page reports must be stapled together before the end of the day
   B. the assignment is to be completed within two hours after it is issued to his subordinates
   C. his subordinates have completed an identical assignment the day before
   D. several entries must be made on a form at varying intervals of time by different clerks

   2.____

3. A supervisor should always remember that the instruction or training of new employees is most effective if it is given when and where it is needed.
   On the basis of this quotation, it is MOST appropriate to conclude that
   A. the new employee should be trained to handle any aspect of his work at the time he starts his job
   B. the new employee should be given the training essential to get him started and additional training when he requires it
   C. an employee who has received excessive training will be just as ineffective as one who has received inadequate training
   D. a new employee is trained most effectively by his own supervisor

   3.____

4. A supervisor may make assignments to his subordinates in the form of a command, a request, or a call for volunteers.
   It is LEAST desirable for a supervisor to make an assignment in the form of a command when
   A. a serious emergency has risen
   B. an employee objects to carrying out an assignment
   C. the assignment must be completed immediately
   D. the assignment is an unpleasant one

   4.____

5. For an office supervisor to confer periodically with his subordinates in order to anticipate job problems which are likely to arise is desirable MAINLY because
   A. there will be fewer problems for which hasty decisions will have to be made
   B. some problems which are anticipated may not arise
   C. his subordinates will learn to refer the problems arising in the unit to him
   D. constant anticipation of future problems tends to raise additional problems

6. As the supervisor of a staff of clerical employees performing various types of work, you are responsible for the accuracy and efficiency with which their work is performed.
   Of the following actions you may take to insure the accuracy of their work, the MOST practical one is for you to
   A. review each operation completed by a staff member before permitting the employee to proceed to the next operation
   B. keep a record of every error made by an employee and use this record to determine whether a careless employee should be transferred or discharged
   C. assign work in such a way that every operation is performed independently by two employees
   D. determine what errors are likely to occur and set up safeguards to prevent the occurrence of these errors

7. One of your subordinates has violated a staff regulation by failing to inform you that he will be absent on a certain day.
   Of the following, the MOST appropriate action for you to take FIRST is to
   A. discuss this matter with your immediate superior
   B. find out the reason for his failure to obey this staff regulation
   C. determine what disciplinary action other supervisors have taken in similar cases
   D. take no action if his absence did not interfere with the work of the unit; reprimand him if it did

8. A newly appointed clerk is assigned to a unit of an agency at a time when the supervisor of the unit is very busy and has little time to devote to instructing the new employee in the work he is to perform.
   Of the following, the MOST appropriate method of training this employee is for the supervisor to
   A. instruct the new employee to observe several experienced clerks at work and question them regarding any aspect of the work he does not understand
   B. delegate the job of training this employee to an employee in the unit who is qualified to instruct him
   C. assign the new employee a simple task and inform him that more complex and varied duties will be given him when the supervisor is less busy
   D. have the employee spend his time reading the agency's annual reports and the laws, rules, and regulations governing its work

9. The channels of communication between the management of a bureau and its employees not only should be kept open and working, but they should also be two-way channels.
Of the following, the MOST effective method for a supervisor to use to carry out this recommendation is to
   A. arrange periodic staff meetings and individual conferences to discuss problems and procedures with his subordinates
   B. change subordinates' assignments regularly so that they will be able to see how their work is related to the objectives of the bureau
   C. issue regular instructions, both written and oral, which clearly show each subordinate's assignments
   D. encourage his subordinates to discuss personal problems with him

10. Work measurement is an essential control tool to an office supervisor.
Of the following, the LEAST important reason for using work measurement as a control tool is that work measurement
   A. may indicate training needs of his subordinates
   B. simplifies the procedures used by the supervisor's subordinates in carrying out their assignments
   C. can indicate whether the supervisor is employing more subordinates than he really needs
   D. is a basis for determining which of the supervisor's subordinates are his most efficient

11. Internal management reporting in agencies is becoming more statistical in nature. Statistics have thus become a major tool in management supervision in agencies.
Before deciding to adopt statistical reporting as a management tool, the management of an agency should FIRST determine whether the
   A. employees of the agency understand the need for, and the use of, statistics in reporting
   B. supervisory staff in the agency is capable of putting reports into statistical form
   C. major activities of the agency can be reported statistically
   D. present achievements of the agency can be compared statistically with those of previous years

12. When assigning work, which of the following criteria would be BEST for a supervisor to use?
   A. Allow each employee to select the tasks he or she does best
   B. Assign all unimportant work to the slower employees
   C. Assign the more tiring tasks to the newer employees
   D. Assign tasks based on the abilities of employees

13. You have been supervising ten people for sixteen months. During that time, your employees have never reported any problems to you.
It is LIKELY that
   A. you are doing such a good job there is no room for improvement

B. since your staff is small, the chances of problems arising are smaller than in a larger unit
C. for some reason your staff is reluctant to discuss problems with you
D. your employees are very competent and are handling all of the problems well by themselves

14. Your supervisor informs you that three of your fifteen employees have complained to her about your inconsistent methods of supervision.
You should
    A. offer to attend a supervisory training program
    B. first ask her if it is proper for her to allow these employees to go over your head
    C. ask her what specific acts have been considered inconsistent
    D. explain that you have purposely been inconsistent because of the needs of these three employees

14.____

15. On short notice, a supervisor must ask her staff to work overtime.
Of the following, it would be BEST to
    A. explain they would be doing her a personal favor which she would appreciate a great deal
    B. explain why it is necessary
    C. reassure them that they can take the time off in the near future
    D. remind them that working overtime occasionally is part of the job requirement

15.____

16. One of your employees has begun reporting to work late on the average of twice a week.
You should
    A. send a memo to everyone in your unit, stressing that lateness cannot be tolerated
    B. privately discuss the matter with the employee to determine if there are any unusual circumstances causing the behavior
    C. bring the issue up at the next staff meeting, without singling out any employee
    D. ask one of your employees to discuss the matter with the individual

16.____

17. One of your employees submitted an application for acceptance into a career development workshop two months ago and has heard nothing. The individual tells you that when one of her co-workers submitted an application, he received a reply a week later.
Which is the BEST response for you to make?
    A. This is obviously a case of discrimination. I'll bring it to the Affirmative Action officer immediately.
    B. Next time you submit a request for something of this nature, let me know and I will write a cover letter that will carry more weight.
    C. Perhaps it was an oversight. Why don't you call the organization and ask why you've heard nothing?
    D. it looks like you won't be accepted this year. Be sure to try again next year.

17.____

18. In order to meet deadlines, a supervisor should
    A. schedule the work and keep informed of its progress
    B. delegate work
    C. hire temporary personnel
    D. know the capabilities of his or her most reliable employees

19. Your supervisor has given instructions to your employees in your absence that differ from those you had given them.
    You should
    A. have your employees follow your instructions
    B. have your employees follow your supervisor's instructions
    C. discuss the matter with your supervisor
    D. discuss the matter with your employees and find out which method they think is best

20. You have found it necessary to return an assignment completed by one of your employees so that several changes can be made. The employee objects to making these changes.
    The MOST appropriate action for you to take FIRST is to
    A. inform the employee that he or she is free to object to your supervisor
    B. ask if the employee has carefully read your proposed changes
    C. calmly state that your decision is final, and further discussion will most likely be useless
    D. allow the employee to present his or her objections against making the changes

21. Among the problems that confront a new supervisor in relation to her or his employees, the one which requires the MOST unusual degree of skill and diplomacy is
    A. changing established ideas
    B. calling attention to mistakes
    C. gaining the respect of employees
    D. training new employees

22. Of the following, the BEST indication of high morale in a supervisor's unit would be the
    A. unit never has to work overtime
    B. supervisor often enjoys staying late to plan work for the following day
    C. unit gives expensive birthday presents to each other
    D. employees are willing to give first priority to attaining group objectives, subordinating personal desires they may have

23. In the satisfactory handling of an employee's complaint which is fancied rather than real, the complaint should be considered
    A. not very important since it has no basis in fact
    B. as important as a grievance grounded in fact
    C. an attempt by the employee to create trouble
    D. an indication of a psychological problem on the part of the employee

24. You are attempting to teach a new employee in your unit how to change a typewriter ribbon. The employee is having a great deal of difficulty changing the ribbon, even though you have always found it simple to do.
Before you spend more time instructing the individual, you should
    A. ask if the employee working nearest would take responsibility for changing the ribbon in the future
    B. tell the employee that you never found this difficult and ask what he or she finds difficult about it
    C. review each of the steps you have already explained and determine whether the individual understands them
    D. tell the employee that you will continue after lunch because you are getting irritable

24._____

25. One of your workers has relatives who raise chickens. One day, you mention in casual conversation that you bought some eggs of poor quality at the grocery store. The following Monday, the worker places a box of fresh eggs on your desk. You thank him and offer to pay, but he refuses. On several occasions thereafter, he brings in additional eggs but still refuses to take payment. He is obviously proud of these products and seems to take great pleasure in sharing them with you. However, you begin to hear rumors that the other workers believe that you and the worker are very friendly and that he is receiving special privileges from you.
You should
    A. explain the situation to the worker, pointing out that he is being hurt by the conditions because of the feelings of others
    B. ignore the situation since the worker is merely being friendly and is actually receiving no favors in return
    C. supervise this worker more carefully than the others to insure that he will not take advantage of the situation
    D. refuse all gifts from the worker thereafter without further explanation

25._____

KEY (CORRECT ANSWERS)

1.	C	11.	C
2.	D	12.	D
3.	B	13.	C
4.	D	14.	C
5.	A	15.	B
6.	D	16.	B
7.	B	17.	C
8.	B	18.	A
9.	A	19.	C
10.	B	20.	D

21. A
22. D
23. B
24. C
25. A

TEST 4

DIRECTIONS: Each question or incomplete statement is followed by several suggested answers or completions. Select the one that BEST answers the question or completes the statement. *PRINT THE LETTER OF THE CORRECT ANSWER IN THE SPACE AT THE RIGHT.*

1. Lax supervision has been blamed largely on the unwillingness of supervisors to supervise their employees.
   The CHIEF reason for this unwillingness to supervise is based MAINLY on the supervisors'
   A. failure to accept modern concepts of proper supervision
   B. doubt of their ability to keep pace with modern techniques and developments in supervision
   C. fear of complaints from employees and the supervisors' wish to avoid unpleasantness
   D. inability to adhere to the same high standards of performance which are required of employees

   1._____

2. The appraisal of employees and their performance is an integral part of the supervisor's job. There is wide agreement that several basic principles must be taken into account by supervisors involved in the appraisal process in order to perform this function correctly.
   The one of the statements below that LEAST represents a basic principle of the appraisal process is:
   A. Appraisals should be based more on performance of definite tasks than on personality considerations.
   B. Appraisal of long-range potential should rely heavily on subjective judgment of that potential.
   C. Appraisal involves the use of value judgments by the supervisor and does, therefore, require reference to pre-established standards.
   D. Appraisal should aim at emphasizing employees' strengths rather than weaknesses.

   2._____

3. Although accuracy and speed are both important in the performance of work, accuracy should be considered more important MAINLY because
   A. most supervisors insist on accurate work
   B. much time is lost in correcting errors
   C. a rapid rate of work cannot be maintained for any length of time
   D. speedy workers are often inaccurate

   3._____

4. If an employee has done a complicated task well, his or her supervisor should
   A. tell the employee that he or she has done a good job
   B. call a staff meeting to see if anyone has suggestions for improving future performance of the task
   C. avoid commending the employee as performing competently is what they are paid to do
   D. confide in the employee that he or she is the best worker in your unit

   4._____

5. You are a newly appointed supervisor in a large office. It had been the practice in that office for the employees to take an unauthorized coffee break at 10:00 A.M. You have been successful in stopping this practice, and for one week no one had gone out for coffee at 10:00 A.M. One day, a stenographer comes over to you at 10:15 A.M., appearing to be ill. She states that she doesn't feel well and that she would like to go out for a cup of tea. She asks your permission to leave the office for a few minutes.
You should
   A. telephone and have a cup of tea delivered to her
   B. permit her to go out
   C. refuse her permission, explaining that you don't wish to set a bad example
   D. tell her she can leave for an early lunch

6. One of the employees you supervise has just put up a small poster in her work area that two of your eight employees find obscene and distasteful. While you don't like the poster either, it doesn't upset you. The two employees already have complained to you about the poster.
Of the following, you should
   A. have the two employees talk to the individual and explain why they are offended
   B. privately explain to the individual that her poster is causing some problems and seek her cooperation in removing it
   C. do nothing as the employee has the right to express her feelings
   D. compromise and allow her to display the poster half of the time

7. One of the most effective ways to build a sense of employee pride, teamwork, and motivation is for the supervisor to seek advice, suggestions, and information from employees concerning ways in which work should be solved. Many experiments in group decision-making have indicated that work groups can help the supervisor in improving decision-making. Where employees feel that they are really part of a team and that they have a significant influence on the decisions that are made, they are more likely to accept the decisions and to seek new solutions to future difficult problems.
According to the above passage, a supervisor should
   A. almost always follow the advice of his or her employees in handling difficult problems
   B. always seek advice from employees when handling difficult problems
   C. choices A and D, but not B
   D. look to employees for assistance in decision-making

8. You have just had a private discussion with the employee with the poster in Question 6 above. You have explained that her poster is causing some problems, and have asked for her cooperation in removing it. She has politely refused to do so, saying, "looking at it cheers her up, and she's been depressed lately."
You should
   A. wait a day or two to see if the incident blows over before deciding whether to take any further action

B. call in the two disgruntled employees within the hour and let them know they'll have to live with the poster as you are not going to act as a censor in the office
C. check agency policies to see if it is legal to have posters down as it is interfering with the work of the unit

9. An employee reprimanded for poor performance tells her supervisor that her recent behavior has been due to a serious family problem. The supervisor suggests several programs which may be able to help her.
The action of the supervisor was
   A. *inappropriate*; the supervisor should not involve herself in the personal affairs of her subordinates
   B. *appropriate*; personal problems frequently affect job performance
   C. *inappropriate*; the employee may consider the supervisor responsible for the subsequent action of the social agencies
   D. *appropriate*; the discussion with the supervisor will in itself tend to solve the problem

9._____

10. Your supervisor informs you that the employee turnover rate in your office is well above the norm and must be reduced.
Which one of the following initial steps would be LEAST appropriate in attempting to overcome this problem?
   A. Decide to be more lenient about the performance standards and about employee requests for time off, so that your office will gain a reputation as a good place to work.
   B. Discuss the problem with a few of your employees whose judgment you trust to see if they can provide insight into the underlying causes of the problem.
   C. Review the records of employees who have left during the past year to see if they can shed some light on the underlying causes of the problem.
   D. Carefully review your training procedures to see if they can be improved

10._____

11. The management principle that each employee should be under the direct control of one immediate supervisor at any one time is known as the principle of
   A. chain of command   B. span of control
   C. unity of command   D. homogeneous assignment

11._____

12. The employees of a unit have been wasteful in the use of office supplies.
Of the following, the MOST desirable action for the supervisor to take to reduce this waste is to
   A. determine the average quantity of supplies used daily by each employee
   B. find out which employees have been most wasteful and reprimand those employees
   C. discuss this matter at a conference with the staff, pointing out the necessity for, and methods of, eliminating waste
   D. issue supplies for an assignment at the time the assignment is made and limit the quantity to the amount needed for that assignment only

12._____

4 (#4)

13. You supervise nineteen employees in a unit which is located directly across from the commissioner's office. One of your new employees has a habit of *showing off* whenever the commissioner is nearby. You have just heard other employees laughing about this behavior among themselves. You like the new employee and would like the employee to be accepted by the others.
Of the following, you should
    A. discuss the situation with two of the older employees and seek their cooperation in being a little more tolerant
    B. talk with the new employee and gently explain the situation
    C. discuss the situation with your most trusted employees and ask them to talk to the others
    D. do nothing

13.____

14. One of your employees comes to you and complains of sexual harassment by your supervisor. The employee has frequently complained about minor issues in the six months she's been there. You have known your supervisor for thirteen years and respect him a great deal. You have known your supervisor for thirteen years and respect him a great deal.
Of the following, you should
    A. firmly let the employee know what a serious allegation she is bringing against your supervisor
    B. let the employee know you will take her concerns seriously
    C. call your supervisor and give him a chance to prepare a defense
    D. inform the employee that she had better have concrete proof for a charge of this nature

14.____

15. The one of the following which is usually the POOREST reason for transferring an employee is to
    A. grant a doctor's request that the employee work nearer to his or her home
    B. take care of changes in workload
    C. relieve the monotony of work assignments

15.____

16. You find that you have unjustly reprimanded one of your subordinates.
You should
    A. ignore the matter, but be more careful in the future
    B. readily admit your mistake to the employee
    C. admit your mistake at your next staff meeting so that your employees will know how fair you are
    D. admit your mistake, but blame the misunderstanding on your supervisor

16.____

17. An experienced, self-confident employee carelessly omitted an essential operation on a job assigned to her. As a result, the completion of an important urgent report was delayed for several hours. A few days later, a relatively inexperienced, sensitive co-worker made a similar careless mistake with similar negative results. The supervisor of the two employees was more gentle in reprimanding the latter than the former employee.

17.____

The supervisor's action in administering reprimands of unequal severity to these two subordinates was
- A. *not appropriate*, because fairness requires that subordinates responsible for like mistakes receive reprimands of like severity
- B. *appropriate*, because supervisors should consider the temperament of subordinates when reprimanding them
- C. *appropriate*, because subordinates who accept greater responsibilities must likewise accept the consequent greater penalties for their mistakes
- D. *not appropriate*, because more experienced employees benefit less, in general, from reprimands than less experienced employees

18. You have just overheard a tense discussion in the cafeteria between two of your best employees. One of them has owed the other $40 for several months and has not paid it back or even mentioned the debt. The employees do not realize that you have heard them.
During that week, you should
    - A. not discuss the matter with either of them
    - B. discuss the matter with both of them, as the conflict may adversely affect their job performance
    - C. discuss the matter with the one who has not paid back the money
    - D. put a clever but meaningful cartoon up on your wall about the importance of paying back debts to friends

19. You have been supervising twenty employees for three months. You suspect that one of your employees, who has worked in the unit longer than anyone else, has perfected the art of looking busy. You wish to find out how much work she is really accomplishing.
Of the following, it would be LEAST appropriate to
    - A. have a frank discussion with the employee about her performance
    - B. set specific time limits on when you would like to get work back from her
    - C. try to observe her more carefully while she is working
    - D. be more careful when monitoring her work output

20. The supervisor of a central files bureau which has fifty employees customarily spends a considerable portion of time in spot-checking the files, reviewing material being transferred from active to inactive files, and similar activities. From the viewpoint of the department management, the MOST pertinent evaluation which can be made on the basis of this information is that the
    - A. supervisor is conscientious and hardworking
    - B. bureau may need additional staff
    - C. supervisor has not made a sufficient delegation of authority and responsibility
    - D. bureau needs an in-service training course as the work of its employees requires an abnormal amount of review

21. You have just been appointed as supervisor of ten employees. The supervisor you are replacing demanded that her subordinate accept their assignments without question. She refused to allow them to exercise initiative in carrying out assignments and maintained a constant check on their work performance.

The MOST appropriate policy for you to adopt would be to
- A. gradually remove the controls you consider too strict and provide opportunities for your staff to participate in formulating work plans and procedures
- B. continue her rigid policies, as the employees are used to this
- C. discontinue all strict controls immediately and give the employees complete freedom in carrying out their assignments
- D. ask your employees what method of supervision they would prefer

22. In any agency, the top administrative officials are concerned largely with the work of overall creative planning with respect to the anticipated progress of the agency. The first-line supervisors, on the other hand, are concerned largely with the control of current action for the execution of current jobs.
On the basis of this quotation, a first-line supervisor would be CHIEFLY responsible for
    - A. increasing or decreasing the responsibilities of his or her unit to reflect changes in the policies of the agency
    - B. modifying the work assignments of his or her present staff to handle a seasonal variation in the activities of the unit
    - C. revising the procedure that is used for transmitting instructions from the head of the agency to the unit heads
    - D. raising and lowering the production goals of his or her unit as often as necessary to adjust them to the abilities of employees

23. As a supervisor, you may find it necessary to consult with your superior before taking action on some matters.
Of the following, the action for which it is MOST important that you obtain the prior approval of your superior is one that involves
    - A. assuming additional functions for your unit
    - B. rotating assignments among your staff members
    - C. initiating regular meetings of your staff
    - D. assigning certain members of your staff to work overtime on an emergency job

24. Suppose that a clerk who is employed in a unit under your supervision performs his work quickly but carelessly. He is about to be transferred to another unit in your department. The chief of this other unit asks you for your opinion of this employee's work habits. The chief of this other unit asks you for your opinion of this employee's work habits.
Of the following, the MOST appropriate reply for you to make is to
    - A. point out this employee's good qualities only since he may correct his bad qualities after his transfer is effected
    - B. say nothing good or bad about this employee, thus permitting him to start his new assignment with a clean slate
    - C. inform the unit chief that this clerk performed his work speedily but was careless
    - D. emphasize his employee's good points and minimize his bad points

25. Of the following, the action that is likely to contribute MOST to the prestige of a supervisor is for him to
    A. expect al his subordinates to perform with equal efficiency any tasks assigned to them
    B. observe the same rules of conduct that he expects his subordinates to observe
    C. seek their advice on his personal problems and offer them his advice on their personal problems
    D. be always frank and outspoken to his subordinates in pointing out their faults

KEY (CORRECT ANSWERS)

1.	C		11.	C
2.	B		12.	C
3.	B		13.	D
4.	A		14.	B
5.	B		15.	D
6.	B		16.	B
7.	D		17.	B
8.	A		18.	A
9.	B		19.	A
10.	A		20.	C

21.	A
22.	B
23.	A
24.	C
25.	C

SUPERVISION, ADMINISTRATION, MANAGEMENT AND ORGANIZATION
EXAMINATION SECTION
TEST 1

DIRECTIONS: Each question or incomplete statement is followed by several suggested answers or completions. Select the one that BEST answers the question or completes the statement. *PRINT THE LETTER OF THE CORRECT ANSWER IN THE SPACE AT THE RIGHT.*

1. The one of the following situations in which you as a supervisor of a group of clerks would probably be able to function MOST effectively from the viewpoint of departmental efficiency is where you are responsible DIRECTLY to
    A. a single supervisor having sole jurisdiction over you
    B. two or three supervisors having coordinate jurisdiction over you
    C. four or five supervisors having coordinate jurisdiction over you
    D. all individuals of higher rank than you in the department

2. Suppose that it is necessary to order one of the clerks under your supervision to stay overtime a few hours one evening. The work to be done is not especially difficult. It is the custom in your office to make such assignments by rotation. The particular clerk whose turn it is to work overtime requests to be excused that evening, but offers to work the next time that overtime is necessary. Hitherto, this clerk has always been very cooperative.
   Of the following, the BEST action for you to take is to
    A. grant the clerk's request, but require her to work overtime two additional nights to compensate for this concession
    B. inform the clerk that you are compelled to refuse any request for special consideration
    C. grant the clerk's request if another clerk is willing to substitute for her
    D. refuse the clerk's request outright because granting her request may encourage her to evade other responsibilities

3. When asked to comment upon the efficiency of Miss Jones, a clerk, her supervisor said, "Since she rarely makes an error, I consider her very efficient."
   Of the following, the MOST valid assumption underlying this supervisor's comment is that
    A. speed and accuracy should be considered separately in evaluating a clerk's efficiency
    B. the most accurate clerks are not necessarily the most efficient
    C. accuracy and competency are directly related
    D. accuracy is largely dependent upon the intelligence of a clerk

4. The one of the following which is the MOST accurate statement of one of the functions of a supervisor is to
   A. select scientifically the person best fitted for the specific job to be done
   B. train the clerks assigned to you in the best methods of doing the work of your office
   C. fit the job to be done to the clerks who are available
   D. assign a clerk only to those tasks for which she has the necessary experience

4.____

5. Assume that you, an experienced supervisor, are given a newly appointed clerk to assist you in performing a certain task. The new clerk presents a method of doing the task which is different from your method but which is obviously better and easy to adopt.
   Of the following you, the supervisor, should
   A. take the suggestion and try it out, even though it was offered by someone less experienced
   B. reject the idea, even though it appears an improvement, as it very likely would not work out
   C. send the new clerk away and get someone else to assist who will be more in accord with your ideas
   D. report him to the head of the office and ask that the new clerk be instructed to do things your way

5.____

6. As a supervisor, you should realize that the one of the following general abilities of a junior clerk which is probably LEAST susceptible to improvement by practice and training is
   A. intelligence   B. speed of typing
   C. knowledge of office procedures   D. accuracy of filing

6.____

7. As a supervisor, when training an employee, you should NOT
   A. correct errors as he makes them
   B. give him too much material to absorb at one time
   C. have him try the operation until he can do it perfectly
   D. treat any foolish question seriously

7.____

8. If a supervisor cannot check readily all the work in her unit, she should
   A. hold up the work until she can personally check it
   B. refuse to take additional work
   C. work overtime until she can personally finish it
   D. delegate part of the work to a qualified subordinate

8.____

9. The one of the following over which a unit supervisor has the LEAST control is
   A. the quality of the work done in his unit
   B. the nature of the work handled in his unit
   C. the morale of workers in his unit
   D. increasing efficiency of his unit

9.____

10. Suppose that you have received a note from an important official in your department commending the work of a unit of clerks under your supervision. Of the following, the BEST action for you to take is to
    A. withhold the note for possible use at a time when the morale of the unit appears to be declining
    B. show the note only to the better members of your staff as a reward for their good work
    C. show the note only to the poorer members of your staff as a stimulus for better work
    D. post the note conspicuously so that it can be seen by all members of your staff

11. If you find that one of your subordinates is becoming apathetic towards his work, you should
    A. prefer charges against him
    B. change the type of work
    C. request his transfer
    D. advise him to take a medical examination to check his health

12. Suppose that a new clerk has been assigned to the unit which you supervise. To give this clerk a brief picture of the functioning of your unit in the entire department would be
    A. *commendable*, because she will probably be able to perform her work with more understanding
    B. *undesirable*, because such action will probably serve only to confuse her
    C. *commendable*, because, if transferred, she would probably be able to work efficiently without additional training
    D. *undesirable*, because in-service training has been demonstrated to be less efficient than on-the-job training

13. Written instructions to a subordinate are of value because they
    A. can be kept up-to-date   B. encourage initiative
    C. make a job seem easier   D. are an aid in training

14. Suppose that you have assigned a task to a clerk under your supervision and have given appropriate instructions. After a reasonable period, you check her work and find that one specific aspect of her work is consistently incorrect. Of the following, the BEST action for you to take is to
    A. determine whether the clerk has correctly understood instructions concerning the aspect of the work not being done correctly
    B. assign the task to a more competent clerk
    C. wait for the clerk to commit a more flagrant error before taking up the matter with her
    D. indicate to the clerk that you are dissatisfied with her work and wait to see whether she is sufficiently intelligent to correct her own mistakes

15. If you wanted to check on the accuracy of the filing in your unit, you would
    A. check all the files thoroughly at regular intervals
    B. watch the clerks while they are filing
    C. glance through filed papers at random
    D. inspect thoroughly a small section of the files selected at random

15._____

16. In making job assignments to his subordinates, a supervisor should follow the principle that each individual generally is capable of
    A. performing one type of work well and less capable of performing other types well
    B. learning to perform a wide variety of different types of work
    C. performing best the type of work in which he has had least experience
    D. learning to perform any type of work in which he is given training

16._____

17. Of the following, the information that is generally considered MOST essential in a departmental organization survey chart is the
    A. detailed operations of the department
    B. lines of authority
    C. relations of the department to other departments
    D. names of the employees of the department

17._____

18. Suppose you are the supervisor in charge of a large unit in which all of the clerical staff perform similar tasks.
    In evaluating the relative accuracy of the clerks, the clerk who should be considered to be the LEAST accurate is the one
    A. whose errors result in the greatest financial loss
    B. whose errors cost the most to locate
    C. who makes the greatest percentage of errors in his work
    D. who makes the greatest number of errors in the unit

18._____

19. Aside from requirements imposed by authority, the frequency with which reports are submitted or the length of the interval which they cover should depend PRINCIPALLY on the
    A. availability of the data to be included in the reports
    B. amount of time required to prepare the reports
    C. extent of the variations in the data with the passage of time
    D. degree of comprehensiveness required in the reports

19._____

20. A serious error has been discovered by a critical superior in work carried on under your supervision.
    It is BEST to explain the situation and prevent its recurrence by
    A. claiming that you are not responsible because you do not check the work personally
    B. accepting the complaint and reporting the name of the employee responsible for the error
    C. assuring him that you hope it will not occur again
    D. assuring him that you will find out how it occurred, so that you can have the work checked with greater care in the future

20._____

21. A serious procedural problem develops in your office.
    In your solution of this problem, the very FIRST step to take is to
    A. select the personnel to help you
    B. analyze your problem
    C. devise the one best method of research
    D. develop an outline of your report

21.____

22. Your office staff consists of eight clerks, stenographers, and typists, cramped in a long narrow room. The room is very difficult to ventilate properly, and, as in so many other offices, the disagreement over the method of ventilation is marked. Two cliques are developing and the friction is carrying over into the work of the office.
    Of the following, the BEST way to proceed is to
    A. call your staff together, have the matter fully discussed giving each person an opportunity to be heard, and put the matter to a vote; then enforce the method of ventilation which has the most votes
    B. call your staff together and have the matter fully discussed. If a compromise arrangement is agreed upon, put it into effect. Otherwise, on the basis of all the facts at your disposal, make a decision as to how best to ventilate the room and enforce your decision
    C. speak to the employees individually, make a decision as to how to ventilate the room, and then enforce your decision
    D. study the layout of the office, make a decision as to how best to ventilate the room, and then enforce your decision

22.____

23. An organization consisting of six levels of authority, where eight persons are assigned to each supervisor on each level, would consist of APPROXIMATELY _____ persons.
    A. 50   B. 500   C. 5,000   D. 50,000

23.____

24. The one of the following which is considered by political scientists to be a GOOD principle of municipal government is
    A. concentration of authority and responsibility
    B. the long ballot
    C. low salaries and a narrow range in salaries
    D. short terms for elected city officials

24.____

25. Of the following, the statement concerning the organization of a department which is TRUE is:
    A. In general, no one employee should have active and constant supervision over more than ten persons.
    B. It is basically unwise to have a supervisor with only three subordinates.
    C. It is desirable that there be no personal contact between the rank and file employee and the supervisor once removed from him.
    D. There should be no more than four levels of authority between the top administrative office in a department and the rank and file employees.

25.____

26. Assuming that Dictaphones are not available, of the following, the situation in which it would be MOST desirable to establish a central stenographic unit is one in which the unit would serve
    A. ten correspondence clerks assigned to full-time positions answering correspondence of a large government department
    B. seven members of a government commission heading a large department
    C. seven heads of bureaus in a government department consisting of 250 employees
    D. fifty investigators in a large department

27. You are assigned to review the procedures in an office in order to recommend improvements to the commissioner directly. You go into an office performing seen routine operations in the processing of one type of office form.
    The question you should FIRST ask yourself in your study of any one of these operations is:
    A. Can it be simplified?
    B. Is it necessary?
    C. Is it performed in proper order or should its position in the procedure be changed?
    D. Is the equipment for doing it satisfactory?

28. You are assigned in charge of a clerical bureau performing a single operation. All five of your subordinates do exactly the same work. A fine spirit of cooperation has developed and the employees help each other and pool their completed work so that the work of any one employee is indistinguishable. Your office is very busy and all five clerks are doing a full day's work. However, reports come back to you from other offices that they are finding as much as 1% error in the work of your bureau. This is too high a percentage of error.
    Of the following, the BEST procedure for you to follow is to
    A. check all the work yourself
    B. have a sample of the work of each clerk checked by another clerk
    C. have all work done in your office checked by one of your clerks
    D. identify the work of each clerk in some way

29. You are put in charge of a small office. In order to cover the office during the lunch hour, you assign Employee A to remain in the office between the hours of 12 and 1 P.M. On your return to the office at 12:25 P.M., you note that no one is in the office and that the phone is ringing. You are forced to postpone your 12:30 P.M. luncheon appointment, and to remain in the office until 12:50 P.M. when Employee A returns to the office.
    The BEST of the following actions is:
    A. Ask Employee why he left the office
    B. Bring charges against Employee A for insubordination and neglect of duty
    C. Ignore the matter in your conversation with Employee A so as not to embarrass him
    D. Make a note to rate Employee A low on his service rating

30. You are assigned in charge of a large division. It had been the practice in that division for the employees to slip out for breakfast about 10:00 A.M. You had been successful in stopping this practice and for one week no one had gone out for breakfast. One day a stenographer comes over to you at 10:30 A.M. appearing to be ill. She states that she doesn't feel well and that she would like to go out for a cup of tea. She asks your permission to leave the office for a few minutes.
You should
    A. telephone and have a cup of tea delivered to her
    B. permit her to go out
    C. refuse her permission to go out inasmuch as this would be setting a bad example
    D. tell her she can leave for an early lunch hour

30._____

31. The following four remarks from a supervisor to a subordinate deal with different situations. One remark, however, implies a basically POOR supervisory practice.
Select this remark as your answer.
    A. "I've called the staff together primarily because I am displeased with the work which one of you is doing. John, don't you think you should be ashamed that you are spoiling the good work of the office?"
    B. "James, you have been with us for six months now. In general, I'm satisfied with your work. However, don't you think you could be more neat in your appearance? I also want you to try to be more accurate in your work."
    C. "Joe, when I assigned this job to you, I did it because it requires special care and I think you're one of our best men in this type of work, but here is a slip-up you've made that we should be especially careful to watch out for in the future."
    D. "Tim, first I'd like to tell you that, effective tomorrow, you are to be my assistant and will receive an increase in salary. Although I recommended you for this position because I felt that you are the best man for the job, there are some things about your work which could stand a bit of improvement. For instance, your manner with regard to visitors is not so polite as it could be."

31._____

32. Of the following, the BEST type of floor surface for an office is
    A. concrete   B. hardwood   C. linoleum   D. parquet

32._____

33. The GENERALLY accepted unit for the measurement of illumination at a desk or work bench is the
    A. ampere   B. foot-candle   C. volt   D. watt

33._____

34. The one of the following who is MOST closely allied with "scientific management" is
    A. Mosher   B. Probst   C. Taylor   D. White

34._____

35. Eliminating slack in work assignments is
    A. speed-up
    B. time study
    C. motion study
    D. efficient management

36. "Time studies" examine and measure
    A. past performance
    B. present performance
    C. long-run effect
    D. influence of change

37. The maximum number of subordinates who can be effectively supervised by one supervisor is BEST considered as
    A. determined by the law of "span of control"
    B. determined by the law of "span of attention"
    C. determined by the type of work supervised
    D. fixed at not more than six

38. In the theory and practice of public administration, the one of the following which is LEAST generally regarded as a staff function is
    A. budgeting
    B. firefighting
    C. purchasing
    D. research and information

39. Suppose you are part of an administrative structure in which the executive head has regularly reporting directly to him seventeen subordinates. To some of the subordinates there regularly report directly three employees, to others four employees, and to the remaining subordinates five employees.
    Called upon to make a suggestion concerning this organization, you would question FIRST the desirability of
    A. so large a variation among the number of employees regularly reporting directly to subordinates
    B. having so large a number of subordinates regularly reporting directly to the administrative head
    C. so small a variation among the number of employees regularly reporting directly to subordinates
    D. the hierarchical arrangement

40. Administration is the center but not necessarily the source of all ideas for procedural improvement.
    The MOST significant implication that this principle bears for the administrative officer is that
    A. before procedural improvements are introduced, they should be approved by a majority of the staff
    B. it is the unique function of the administrative officer to derive and introduce procedural improvements
    C. the administrative office should derive ideas and suggestions for procedural improvement from all possible sources, introducing any that promise to be effective
    D. the administrative officer should view employee grievances as the chief source of procedural improvements

9 (#1)

41. The merit system should not end with the appointment of a candidate. In any worthy public service system there should be no dead-end jobs. If the best citizen is to be attracted to public service, there must be provided encouragement and incentive to enable such a career employee to progress in the service.
The one of the following which is the MOST accurate statement on the basis of the above statement is that
   A. merit system selection has replaced political appointment in many governmental units
   B. lack of opportunities for advancement in government employment will discourage the better qualified from applying
   C. employees who want to progress in the public service should avoid simple assignments
   D. most dead-end jobs have been eliminated from the public service

41.____

42. Frequently the importance of keeping office records is not appreciated until information which is badly needed cannot be found. Office records must be kept in convenient and legible form, and must be filed where they may be found quickly. Many clerks are required for this work in large offices and fixed standards of accomplishment often can and must be utilized to get the desired results without loss of time.
The one of the following which is the MOST accurate statement on the basis of the above statement is:
   A. In setting up a filing system, the system to be used is secondary to the purpose it is to serve.
   B. Office records to be valuable must be kept in duplicate.
   C. The application of work standards to certain clerical functions frequently leads to greater efficiency.
   D. The keeping of office records becomes increasingly important as the business transacted by an office grows.

42.____

43. The difference between the average worker and the expert in any occupation is to a large degree a matter of training, yet the difference in their output is enormous. Despite this fact, there are many offices which do not have any organized system of training.
The MOST accurate of the following statements on the basis of the above statement is that
   A. job training, to be valuable, should be a continuous process
   B. most clerks have the same general intelligence but differ only in the amount of training they have received
   C. skill in an occupation can be acquired as a result of instruction by others
   D. employees with similar training will produce similar quality and quantity of work

43.____

44. Sometimes the term "clerical work" is used synonymously with the term "office work" to indicate that the work is clerical work, whether done by a clerk in a place called "the office," by the foreman in the shop, or by an investigator in the field. The essential feature is the work itself, not who does it or where it is done. If it is clerical work in one place, it is clerical work everywhere.

44.____

Of the following, the LEAST DIRECT implication of the above statement is that
- A. many jobs have clerical aspects
- B. some clerical work is done in offices
- C. the term "clerical work" is used in place of the term "office work" to emphasize the nature of the work done rather than by whom it is done
- D. clerks are not called upon to perform other than clerical work

45. Scheduling work within a unit involves the knowledge of how long the component parts of the routine take, and the precedence which certain routines should take over others. Usually, the important functions should be attended to on a schedule, and less important work can be handled as fill-in.
The one of the following which is the VALID statement on the basis of the above statement is that
- A. only employees engaged in routine assignments should have their work scheduled
- B. the work of an employee should be so scheduled that occasional absences will not upset his routine
- C. a proper scheduling of work takes the importance of the various functions of a unit into consideration
- D. if office work is not properly scheduled, important functions will be neglected

46. A filing system is unquestionably an effective tool for the systematic executive, and it use in office practice is indispensable, but a casual examination of almost any filing drawer in any office will show that hundreds of letters and papers which have no value whatever are being preserved.
The LEAST accurate of the following statements on the basis of the above statement is that
- A. it is generally considered to be good office practice to destroy letters or papers which are of no value
- B. many files are cluttered with useless paper
- C. a filing system is a valuable aid in effective office management
- D. every office executive should personally make a thorough examination of the files at regular intervals

47. As a supervisor, you may receive requests for information which you know should not be divulged.
Of the following replies you may give to such a request received over the telephone, the BEST one is:
- A. "I regret to advise you that it is the policy of the department not to give out this information over the telephone."
- B. "If you hold on a moment, I'll have you connected with the chief of the division."
- C. "I am sorry that I cannot help you, but we are not permitted to give out any information regarding such matters."
- D. "I am sorry but I know nothing regarding this matter."

48. Training promotes cooperation and teamwork, and results in lowered unit costs of operation.
The one of the following which is the MOST valid implication of the above statement is that
   A. training is of most value to new employees
   B. training is a factor in increasing efficiency and morale
   C. the actual cost of training employees may be small
   D. training is unnecessary in offices where personnel costs cannot be reduced

49. A government employee should understand how his particular duties contribute to the achievement of the objectives of his department.
This statement means MOST NEARLY that
   A. an employee who understands the functions of his department will perform his work efficiently
   B. all employees contribute equally in carrying out the objectives of their department
   C. an employee should realize the significance of his work in relation to the aims of his department
   D. all employees should be able to assist in setting up the objectives of a department

50. Many office managers have a tendency to overuse form letters and are prone to print form letters for every occasion, regardless of the number of copies of these letters which is needed.
On the basis of this statement, it is MOST logical to state that the determination of the need for a form letter should depend upon the
   A. length of the period during which the form letter may be used
   B. number of form letters presently being used in the office
   C. frequency with which the form letter may be used
   D. number of typists who may use the form letter

KEY (CORRECT ANSWERS)

1.	A	11.	B	21.	B	31.	A	41.	B
2.	C	12.	A	22.	B	32.	C	42.	C
3.	C	13.	D	23.	A	33.	B	43.	C
4.	B	14.	A	24.	A	34.	C	44.	D
5.	A	15.	D	25.	D	35.	D	45.	C
6.	A	16.	B	26.	D	36.	B	46.	D
7.	B	17.	B	27.	B	37.	C	47.	C
8.	D	18.	C	28.	D	38.	B	48.	B
9.	B	19.	C	29.	A	39.	B	49.	C
10.	D	20.	D	30.	B	40.	C	50.	C

TEST 2

DIRECTIONS: Each question or incomplete statement is followed by several suggested answers or completions. Select the one that BEST answers the question or completes the statement. *PRINT THE LETTER OF THE CORRECT ANSWER IN THE SPACE AT THE RIGHT.*

1. Your bureau is assigned an important task.
   Of the following, the function that you, as an administrative officer, can LEAST reasonably be expected to perform under these circumstances is the
   A. division of the large job into individual tasks
   B. establishment of "production lines" within the bureau
   C. performance personally of a substantial share of all the work
   D. checkup to see that the work has been well done

   1.____

2. Suppose that you have broken a complex job into its smaller components before making assignments to the employees under your jurisdiction.
   Of the following, the LEAST advisable procedure to follow from that point is to
   A. give each employee a picture of the importance of his work for the success of the total job
   B. establish a definite line of work flow and responsibility
   C. post a written memorandum of the best method for performing each job
   D. teach a number of alternative methods for doing each job

   2.____

3. As an administrative officer, you are requested to draw up an organization chart of the whole department.
   Of the following, the MOST important characteristic of such a chart is that it will
   A. include all details of the organization which distinguish it from any other
   B. be a schematic representation of purely administrative functions within the department
   C. present a modification of the actual departmental organization in light of principles of scientific management
   D. present an accurate picture of the lines of authority and responsibility

   3.____

4. Of the following, the MOST important principle in respect to delegation of authority that should guide you in your work as supervisor in charge of a bureau is that you should
   A. delegate as much authority as you effectively can
   B. make certain that all administrative details clear through your desk
   C. have all decisions confirmed by you
   D. discourage the practice of consulting you on matters of basic policy

   4.____

5. Of the following, the LEAST valid criterion to be applied in evaluating the organization of the department in which you are employed as a supervisor is:
   A. Is authority for making decisions centralized?
   B. Is authority for formulating policy centralized?
   C. Is authority granted commensurate with the responsibility involved?
   D. Is each position and its relation to other positions from the standpoint of responsibility clearly defined?

   5.____

6. Functional centralization is the bringing together of employees doing the same kind of work and performing similar tasks.
Of the following, the one which is NOT an important advantage flowing from the introduction of functional centralization in a large city department is that
   A. inter-bureau communication and traffic are reduced
   B. standardized work procedures are introduced more easily
   C. evaluation of employee performances is facilitated
   D. inequalities in working conditions are reduced

7. As a supervisor, you find that a probationary employee under your supervision is consistently below a reasonable standard of performance for the job he is assigned to do.
Of the following, the MOST appropriate action for you to take FIRST is to
   A. give him an easier job to do
   B. advise him to transfer to another department
   C. recommend to your superior that he be discouraged at the end of his probationary period
   D. determine whether the cause for his below-standard performance can be readily remedied

8. Certain administrative functions, such as those concerned with budgetary and personnel selection activities, have been delegated to central agencies separated from the operating departments.
Of the following, the PRINCIPAL reason for such separation is that
   A. a central agency is generally better able to secure funds for performing these functions
   B. decentralization increases executive control
   C. greater economy, efficiency, and uniformity can be obtained by establishing central staff of experts to perform these functions
   D. the problems involved in performing these functions vary significantly from one operating department to another

9. The one of the following which is LEAST valid as a guiding principle for you, in your work as supervisor, in building team spirit and teamwork in your bureau is that you should attempt to
   A. convince the personnel of the bureau that public administration is a worthwhile endeavor
   B. lead every employee to visualize the integration of his own individual function with the program of the whole bureau
   C. develop a favorable public attitude toward the work of the bureau
   D. maintain impartiality by convenient delegation of authority in controversial matters

10. Of the following, the LEAST desirable procedure for the competent supervisor to follow is to
    A. organize his work before taking responsibility for helping others with theirs
    B. avoid schedules and routines when he is busy
    C. be flexible in planning and carrying out his responsibilities
    D. secure the support of his staff in organizing the total job of the unit

11. The responsibility for making judgment about staff members which is inherent in the supervisor's position may arouse hostilies toward the supervisor.
    Of the following, the BEST suggestion to the supervisor for handling this responsibility is for the supervisor to avoid
    A. individual criticism by taking up problems directly through group meetings
    B. any personal feeling or action that would imply that the supervisor has any power over the staff
    C. making critical judgments without accompanying them with reassurance to the staff member concerned

11.____

12. To carry out MOST effectively his responsibility for holding to a standard of quantity and quality, the supervisor should
    A. demand much more from himself than he does from his staff
    B. provide a clearly defined statement of what is expected of the staff
    C. teach the staff to assume responsible attitudes
    D. help the staff out when they get into unavoidable difficulties

12.____

13. The supervisor should inspire confidence and respect.
    This objective is MOST likely to be attained by the supervisor if he endeavors always to
    A. know the answers to the workers' questions
    B. be fair and just
    C. know what is going on in the office
    D. behave like a supervisor

13.____

14. Two chief reasons for the centralization of office functions are to eliminate costly duplication and to bring about greater coordination.
    The MOST direct implication of this statement is that
    A. greater coordination of office work will result in centralization of office functions
    B. where there is no centralization of office functions, there can be no coordination of work
    C. centralization of office functions may reduce duplication of work
    D. decentralization of office functions may be a result of costly duplication

14.____

15. The efficient administrative assistant arranges a definite schedule of the regular work of his division, but assigns the occasional and emergency tasks when they arise to the employees available at the time to handle these tasks.
    The management procedure described in this statement is desirable MAINLY because it
    A. relieves the administrative assistant of the responsibility of supervising the work of his staff
    B. enables more of the staff to become experienced in handling different types of problems
    C. enables the administrative assistant to anticipate problems which may arise
    D. provides for consideration of current work load when making special assignments

15.____

16. Well-organized training courses for office employees are regarded by most administrators as a fundamental and essential part of a well-balanced personnel program.
    Such training of clerical employees results LEAST directly in
    A. providing a reservoir of trained employees who can carry on the duties of other clerks during the absence of these clerks
    B. reducing the individual differences in the innate ability of clerical employees to perform complex duties
    C. bringing about a standardization throughout the department of operational methods found to be highly effective in one of its units
    D. preparing clerical employees for promotion to more responsible positions

17. The average typing speed of a typist is not necessarily a true indication of her efficiency.
    Of the following, the BEST justification for this statement is that
    A. the typist may not maintain her maximum typing speed at all times
    B. a rapid typist will ordinarily type more letters than a slow one
    C. a typist's assignments usually include other operations in addition to actual typing
    D. typing speed has no significant relationship to the difficulty of material being typed

18. Although the use of labor-saving machinery and the simplification of procedures tend to decrease unit clerical labor costs, there is, nevertheless, a contrary tendency in the overall cost of office work. This contrary tendency, evidenced by the increase in size of the office staffs, has developed from the increasingly extensive use of systems of analysis and methods of research.
    Of the following, the MOST accurate statement on the basis of the above statement is that
    A. the tendency for the overall costs of office work to increase is bringing about a counter-tendency to decrease unit costs of office work
    B. office machines are of little value in reducing the unit costs of the work of offices in which the overall costs are increasing
    C. The increasing use of systems of analysis and methods of research is bringing about a condition which will necessitate a curtailment of the use of these techniques in the office
    D. expanded office functions tend to offset savings resulting from increased efficiency in office management

19. The most successful supervisor wins his victories through preventive rather than through curative action.
    The one of the following which is the MOST accurate statement on the basis of this statement is that
    A. success in supervision may be measured more accurately in terms of errors corrected than in terms of errors prevented
    B. anticipating problems makes for better supervision than waiting until these problems arise

C. difficulties that cannot be prevented by the supervisor cannot be overcome
D. the solution of problems in supervision is best achieved by scientific methods

20. Assume that you have been requested to design an office form which is to be duplicated by the mimeograph process.
In planning the layout of the various items appearing on the form, it is LEAST important for you to know the
   A. amount of information which the form is to contain
   B. purpose for which the form will be used
   C. size of the form
   D. number of copies of the form which are required

21. The supervisor is responsible for the accuracy of the work performed by her subordinates.
Of the following procedures which she might adopt to insure the accurate copying of long reports from rough draft originals, the MOST effective one is to
   A. examine the rough draft for errors in grammar, punctuation, and spelling before assigning it to a typist to copy
   B. glance through each typed report before it leaves her bureau to detect any obvious errors made by the typist
   C. have another employee read the rough draft original to the typist who typed the report, and have the typist make whatever corrections are necessary
   D. rotate assignments involving the typing of long reports equally among all the typists in the unit

22. The total number of errors made during the month, or other period studied, indicates, in a general way, whether the work has been performed with reasonable accuracy. However, this is not in itself a true measure, but must be considered in relation to the total volume of work produced.
On the basis of this statement, the accuracy of work performed is MOST truly measured by the
   A. total number of errors made during a specified period
   B. comparison of the number of errors made and the quantity of work produced during a specified period
   C. average amount of work produced by the unit during each month or other designated period of time
   D. none of the above answers

23. In the course of your duties, you receive a letter which, you believe, should be called to the attention of your supervisor.
Of the following, the BEST reason for attaching previous correspondence to this letter before giving it to your supervisor is that
   A. there is less danger, if such a procedure is followed, of misplacing important letters
   B. this letter can probably be better understood in the light of previous correspondence

C. your supervisor is probably in a better position to understand the letter than you
D. this letter will have to be filed eventually so there is no additional work involved

24. Suppose that you are requested to transmit to the stenographers in your bureau an order curtailing certain privileges that they have been enjoying. You anticipate that your staff may resent curtailment of such privileges.
Of the following, the BEST action for you to take is to
   A. impress upon your staff that an order is an order and must be obeyed
   B. attempt to explain to your staff the probable reasons for curtailing their privileges
   C. excuse the curtailment of privileges by saying that the welfare of the staff was evidently not considered
   D. warn your staff that violation of an order may be considered sufficient cause for immediate dismissal

24.____

25. Suppose that a stenographer recently appointed to your bureau submits a memorandum suggesting a change in office procedure that has been tried before and has been found unsuccessful.
Of the following, the BEST action for you to take is to
   A. send the stenographer a note acknowledging receipt of the suggestion, but do not attempt to carry out the suggestion
   B. point out that suggestions should come from her supervisor, who has a better knowledge of the problems of the office
   C. try out the suggested change a second time, lest the stenographer lose interest in her work
   D. call the stenographer in, explain that the change if not practicable, and compliment her for her interest and alertness

25.____

26. Suppose that you are assistant to one of the important administrators in your department. You receive a note from the head of department asking your supervisor to assist with a pressing problem that has arisen by making an immediate recommendation. Your supervisor is out of town on official business for a few days and cannot be reached. The head of department, evidently, is not aware of his absence.
Of the following, the BEST action for you to take is to
   A. send the note back to the head of department without comment so as not to incriminate your supervisor
   B. forward the note to one of the administrators in another division of the department
   C. wait until your supervisor returns and bring the note to his attention immediately
   D. get in touch with the head of department immediately and inform him that your supervisor is out of town

26.____

27. One of your duties may be to estimate the budget of your unit for the next fiscal year. Suppose that you expect no important changes in the work of your unit during the next year.

27.____

Of the following, the MOST appropriate basis for estimating next year's budget is the
- A. average budget of your unit for the last five years
- B. budget of your unit for the current year plus fifty percent to allow for possible expansion
- C. average current budget of units in your department
- D. budget of your unit for the current fiscal year

28. As a supervisor, you should realize that the work of a stenographer ordinarily requires a higher level of intelligence than the work of a typist CHIEFLY because
    - A. the salary range of stenographers is, in most government and business offices, lower than the salary range of typists
    - B. greater accuracy and skill is ordinarily required of a typist
    - C. the stenographer must understand what is being dictated to enable her to write it out in shorthand
    - D. typists are required to do more technical and specialized work

29. Suppose that you are acting as assistant to an important administrator in your department.
    Of the following, the BEST reason for keeping a separate "pending" file of letters to which answers are expected very soon is that
    - A. important correspondence should be placed in a separate, readily accessible file
    - B. a periodic check of the "pending" file will indicate the possible need for follow-up letters
    - C. correspondence is never final, so provision should be made for keeping files open
    - D. there is seldom sufficient room in the permanent files to permit filing all letters

30. For a busy executive in a government department, the services of an assistant are valuable and almost indispensable.
    Of the following, the CHIEF value of an assistant PROBABLY lies in her
    - A. ability to assume responsibility for making major decisions
    - B. familiarity with the general purpose and functions of civil service
    - C. special education
    - D. familiarity with the work and detail involved in the duties of the executive whom she assists

31. The supervisor should set a good example.
    Of the following, the CHIEF implication of the above statement is that the supervisor should
    - A. behave as he expects his workers to behave
    - B. know as much about the worker as his workers do
    - C. keep his workers informed of what he is doing
    - D. keep ahead of his workers

32. Of the following, the LEAST desirable procedure for the competent supervisor to follow is to
    A. organize his work before taking responsibility for helping others with theirs
    B. avoid schedules and routines when he is busy
    C. be flexible in planning and carrying out his responsibilities
    D. secure the support of his staff in organizing the total job of the unit

33. Evaluation helps the worker by increasing his security.
    Of the following, the BEST justification for this statement is that
    A. security and growth depend upon knowledge by the worker of the agency's evaluation
    B. knowledge of his evaluation by agency and supervisor will stimulate the worker to better performance
    C. evaluation enables the supervisor and worker to determine the reasons for the worker's strengths and weaknesses
    D. the supervisor and worker together can usually recognize and deal with any worker's insecurity

34. Systematizing for efficiency means MOST NEARLY
    A. performing an assignment despite all interruptions
    B. leaving difficult assignments until the next day
    C. having a definite time schedule for certain daily duties
    D. trying to do as little work as possible

35. The CHIEF reason for an employee training program is to
    A. increase the efficiency of the employee's work
    B. train the employee for promotion examinations
    C. to meet and talk with each new employee
    D. to give the supervisor an opportunity to reprimand the employee for his lack of knowledge

36. A supervisor may encourage his subordinates to make suggestions by
    A. keeping a record of the number of suggestions an employee makes
    B. providing a suggestion box
    C. outlining a list of possible suggestions
    D. giving credit to a subordinate whose suggestion has been accepted and used

37. The statement that accuracy is of greater importation than speed means MOST NEARLY that
    A. slower work increases employment
    B. fast workers may be inferior workers
    C. there are many varieties of work to do in an office
    D. the slow worker is the most efficient person

38. To print tabular material is always much more expensive than to print straight text.
It follows MOST NEARLY that
   A. the more columns and subdivisions there are in a table, the more expensive is the printing
   B. the omission of the number and title from a table reduces printing costs
   C. it is always desirable to only print straight text
   D. do not print tabular material as it is too expensive

39. If you were required to give service ratings to employees under your supervision, you should consider as MOST important, during the current period, the
   A. personal characteristics and salary and grade of an employee
   B. length of service and the volume of work performed
   C. previous service rating given him
   D. personal characteristics and the quality of work of an employee

40. If a representative committee of employees in a large department is to meet with an administrative officer for the purpose of improving staff relations and of handling grievances, it is BEST that these meetings be held
   A. at regular intervals
   B. whenever requested b an aggrieved employee
   C. whenever the need arises
   D. at the discretion of the administrative officer

41. In order to be best able to teach a newly appointed employee who must learn to do a type of work which is unfamiliar to him, his supervisor should realize that during this first stage in the learning process the subordinate is GENERALLY characterized by
   A. acute consciousness of self
   B. acute consciousness of subject matter, with little interest in persons or personalities
   C. inertness or passive acceptance of assigned role
   D. understanding of problems without understanding of the means of solving them

42. The MOST accurate of the following principles of education and learning for a supervisor to keep in mind when planning a training program for the assistant supervisors under her supervision is that
   A. assistant supervisors, like all other individuals, vary in the rate at which they learn new material and in the degree to which they can retain what they do learn
   B. experienced assistant supervisors who have the same basic college education and agency experience will be able to learn new material at approximately the same rate of speed
   C. the speed with which assistant supervisors can learn new material after the age of forty is half as rapid as at ages twenty to thirty
   D. with regard to any specific task, it is easier and takes less time to break an experienced assistant supervisor of old, unsatisfactory work habits than it is to teach him new, acceptable ones

43. A supervisor has been transferred from supervision of one group of units to another group of units in the same center. She spends the first three weeks in her new assignment in getting acquainted with her new subordinates, their caseload problems and their work. In this process, she notices that some of the cash records and forms which are submitted to her by two of the assistant supervisors are carelessly or improperly prepared.
The BEST of the following actions for the supervisor to take in this situation is to
    A. carefully check the work submitted by these assistant supervisors during an additional three weeks before taking any more positive action
    B. confer with these offending workers and show each one where her work needs improvement and how to go about achieving it
    C. institute an in-service training program specifically designed to solve such a problem and instruct the entire subordinate staff in proper work methods
    D. make a note of these errors for documentary use in preparing the annual service rating reports and advise the workers involved to prepare their work more carefully

43._____

44. A supervisor, who was promoted to this position a year ago, has supervised a certain assistant supervisor for this one year. The work of the assistant supervisor has been very poor because he has done a minimum of work, refused to take sufficient responsibility, been difficult to handle, and required very close supervision. Apparently due to the increasing insistence by his supervisor that he improve the caliber of his work, the assistant supervisor tenders his resignation, stating that the demands of the job are too much for him. The opinion of the previous supervisor, who had supervised this assistant supervisor for two years, agrees substantially with that of the new supervisor. Under such circumstances, the BEST of the following actions the supervisor can take, in general, is to
    A. recommend that the resignation be accepted and that he be rehired should he later apply when he feels able to do the job
    B. recommend that the resignation be accepted and that he not be rehired should he later so apply
    C. refuse to accept the resignation but try to persuade the assistant supervisor to accept psychiatric help
    D. refuse to accept the resignation, promising the assistant supervisor that he will be less closely supervised in the future since he is now so experienced

44._____

45. Rumors have arisen to the effect that one of the staff investigators under your supervision has been attending classes at a local university during afternoon hours when he is supposed to be making field visits.
The BEST of the following ways for you to approach this problem is to
    A. disregard the rumors since, like most rumors, they probably have no actual foundation in fact
    B. have a discreet investigation made in order to determine the actual facts prior to taking any other action

45._____

11 (#2)

    C. inform the investigator that you know what he has been doing and that such behavior is overt dereliction of duty and is punishable by dismissal
    D. review the investigator's work record, spot check his cases, and take no further action unless the quality of his work is below average for the unit

46. A supervisor must consider many factors in evaluating a worker whom he has supervised for a considerable time.
In evaluating the capacity of such a worker to use independent judgment, the one of the following to which the supervisor should generally give MOST consideration is the worker's
    A. capacity to establish good relationships with people (clients, colleagues)
    B. educational background
    C. emotional stability
    D. the quality and judgment shown by the worker in previous work situations known to the supervisor

46.____

47. A supervisor is conducting a special meeting with the assistant supervisors under her supervision to read and discuss some major complex changes in the rules and procedures. She notices that one of the assistant supervisors who is normally attentive at meetings seems to be paying no attention to what is being said. The supervisor stops reading the rules and asks the assistant supervisor a couple of questions about the changed procedure, to which she gets satisfactory answers.
The BEST action of the following for the supervisor to take at the meeting is to
    A. advise the assistant supervisor gently but firmly that these changes are complex and that her undivided attention is required in order to fully comprehend them
    B. avoid further embarrassment to the assistant supervisor by asking the group as a whole to pay more attention to what is being read
    C. discontinue the questioning and resume reading the procedure
    D. politely request the assistant supervisor to stop giving those present the impression that she is uninterested in what goes on about her

47.____

48. A supervisor becomes aware that one of her very competent experienced workers never takes notes during an interview with a client except to note an occasional name, address, or date. When asked about this practice by the supervisor, the worker states that she has a good memory for important details and has always been able to satisfactorily record an interview after the client has left.
It would generally be BEST for the supervisor to handle this situation by
    A. discussing with her that more extensive note-taking may sometimes be desirable with a client who believes note-taking to be evidence that his problem will receive serious consideration
    B. agreeing with this practice since note-taking interferes with the establishment of a proper worker-client relationship
    C. explaining that, since interviewing is an art form rather than an exact science, a good worker must devise her own personal rules for interviewing and not be bound by general principles

48.____

D. warning the worker that memory is too uncertain a thing to be relied upon and, therefore, notes should be taken during an interview of all matters

49. When an experienced subordinate who has the authority and information necessary to make a decision on a certain difficult matter brings the matter to his supervisor without having made the decision, it would generally be BEST for the supervisor to
    A. agree to make the decision for the subordinate after the subordinate has explained why he finds it difficult to make the decision and after he has made a recommendation
    B. make the decision for the subordinate, explaining to him the reasons for arriving at the decision
    C. refuse to make the decision, but discuss the various alternatives with the subordinate in order to clarify the issues involved
    D. refuse to make the decision, explaining to the subordinate that he is deemed to be fully qualified and competent to make the decision

49.____

50. The one of the following instances when it is MOST important for an upper level supervisor to follow the chain of command is when he is
    A. communicating decisions   B. communicating information
    C. receiving suggestions   D. seeking information

50.____

KEY (CORRECT ANSWERS)

1.	C	11.	D	21.	C	31.	A	41.	A
2.	D	12.	B	22.	B	32.	B	42.	A
3.	D	13.	B	23.	B	33.	C	43.	B
4.	A	14.	C	24.	B	34.	C	44.	B
5.	D	15.	D	25.	D	35.	A	45.	B
6.	A	16.	B	26.	D	36.	D	46.	D
7.	D	17.	C	27.	D	37.	B	47.	C
8.	C	18.	D	28.	C	38.	A	48.	A
9.	D	19.	B	29.	B	39.	D	49.	C
10.	B	20.	D	30.	D	40.	A	50.	A

TEST 3

DIRECTIONS: Each question or incomplete statement is followed by several suggested answers or completions. Select the one that BEST answers the question or completes the statement. *PRINT THE LETTER OF THE CORRECT ANSWER IN THE SPACE AT THE RIGHT.*

1. Experts in the field of personnel relations feel that it is generally bad practice for subordinate employees to become aware of pending or contemplated changes in policy or organizational set-up via the "grapevine" CHIEFLY because 1.____
   A. evidence that one or more responsible officials have proved untrustworthy will undermine confidence in the agency
   B. the information disseminated by this method is seldom entirely accurate and generally spreads needless unrest among the subordinate staff
   C. the subordinate staff may conclude that the administration feels the staff cannot be trusted with the true information
   D. the subordinate staff may conclude that the administration lacks the courage to make an unpopular announcement through officials channels

2. In order to maintain a proper relationship with a worker who is assigned to staff rather than line functions, a line supervisor should 2.____
   A. accept all recommendations of the staff worker
   B. include the staff worker in the conferences called by the supervisor for his subordinates
   C. keep the staff worker informed of developments in the area of his staff assignment
   D. require that the staff worker's recommendations be communicated to the supervisor through the supervisor's own superior

3. Of the following, the GREATEST disadvantage of placing a worker in a staff position under the direct supervision of the supervisor whom he advises is the possibility that the 3.____
   A. staff worker will tend to be insubordinate because of a feeling of superiority over the supervisor
   B. staff worker will tend to give advice of the type which the supervisor wants to hear or finds acceptable
   C. supervisor will tend to be mistrustful of the advice of a worker of subordinate rank
   D. supervisor will tend to derive little benefit from the advice because to supervise properly he should know at least as much as his subordinate

4. One factor which might be given consideration in deciding upon the optimum span of control of a supervisor over his immediate subordinates is the position of the supervisor in the hierarchy of the organization. It is generally considered proper that the number of subordinates immediately supervised by a higher, upper echelon, supervisor 4.____
   A. is unrelated to and tends to form no pattern with the number supervised by lower level supervisors
   B. should be about the same as the number supervised by a lower level supervisor

C. should be larger than the number supervised by a lower level supervisor
D. should be smaller than the number supervised by a lower level supervisor

5. An important administrative problem is how precisely to define the limits on authority that is delegated to subordinate supervisors.
Such definition of limits of authority should be
   A. as precise as possible and practicable in all areas
   B. as precise as possible and practicable in areas of function, but should allow considerable flexibility in the area of personnel management
   C. as precise as possible and practicable in the area of personnel management, but should allow considerable flexibility in the areas of function
   D. in general terms so as to allow considerable flexibility both in the areas of function and in the areas of personnel management

6. The LEAST important of the following reasons why a particular activity should be assigned to a unit which performs activities dissimilar to it is that
   A. close coordination is needed between the particular activity and other activities performed by the unit
   B. it will enhance the reputation and prestige of the unit supervisor
   C. the unit makes frequent use of the results of this particular activity
   D. the unit supervisor has a sound knowledge and understanding of the particular activity

7. A supervisor is put in charge of a special unit. She is exceptionally well-qualified for this assignment by her training and experience. One of her very close personal friends has been working for some time as a field investigator in this unit. Both the supervisor and investigator are certain that the rest of the investigators in the unit, many of whom have been in the bureau for a long time, know of this close relationship.
Under these circumstances, the MOST advisable action for the supervisor to take is to
   A. ask that either she be allowed to return to her old assignment, or, if that cannot be arranged, that her friend be transferred to another unit in the center
   B. avoid any overt sign of favoritism by acting impartially and with greater reserve when dealing with this investigator than the rest of the staff
   C. discontinue any socializing with this investigator either inside or outside the office so as to eliminate any gossip or dissatisfaction
   D. talk the situation over with the other investigators and arrive at a mutually acceptable plan of proper office decorum

8. The one of the following causes of clerical error which is usually considered to be LEAST attributable to faulty supervision or inefficient management is
   A. inability to carry out instructions
   B. too much work to do
   C. an inappropriate record-keeping system
   D. continual interruptions

9. Assume that you are the supervisor of a clerical unit in a government agency. One of your subordinates violates a rule of the agency, a violation which requires that the employee be suspended from his work for one day. The violated rule is one that you have found to be unduly strict and you have recommended to the management of the agency that the rule be changed or abolished. The management has been considering your recommendation but has not yet reached a decision on the matter.
In these circumstances, you should
   A. not initiate disciplinary action, but, instead explain to the employee that the rule may be changed shortly
   B. delay disciplinary action on the violation until the management has reached a decision on changing the rule
   C. modify the disciplinary action by reprimanding the employee and informing him that further action may be taken when the management has reached a decision on changing the rule
   D. initiate the prescribed disciplinary action without commenting on the strictness of the rule or on your recommendation

10. Assume that a supervisor praises his subordinates for satisfactory aspects of their work only when he is about to criticize them for unsatisfactory aspects of their work.
Such a practice is undesirable PRIMARILY because
   A. his subordinates may expect to be praised for their work even if it is unsatisfactory
   B. praising his subordinates for some aspects of their work while criticizing other aspects will weaken the effects of the criticisms
   C. his subordinates would be more receptive to criticism if it were followed by praise
   D. his subordinates may come to disregard praise and wait for criticism to be given

11. The one of the following which would be the BEST reason for an agency to eliminate a procedure for obtaining and recording certain information is that
   A. it is no longer legally required to obtain the information
   B. there is an advantage in obtaining the information
   C. the information could be compiled on the basis of other information available
   D. the information obtained is sometimes incorrect

12. In determining the type and number of records to be kept in an agency, it is important to recognize that records are of value PRIMARILY as
   A. raw material to be used in statistical analysis
   B. sources of information about the agency's activities
   C. by-products of the activities carried on by the agency
   D. data for evaluating the effectiveness of the agency

Questions 13-17.

DIRECTIONS: Each of Questions 13 through 17 consists of a statement which contains one word that is incorrectly used because it is not in keeping with the meaning that the statement is evidently intended to convey. For each of these questions, you are to select the incorrectly used word and substitute for it one of the words lettered A, B, C, or D, which helps BEST to convey the meaning of the statement.

13. There has developed in recent years an increasing awareness of the need to measure the quality of management in all enterprises and to seek the principles that can serve as a basis for this improvement. 13._____
    A. growth   B. raise   C. efficiency   D. define

14. It is hardly an exaggeration to deny that the permanence, productivity, and humanity of any industrial system depend upon its ability to utilize the positive and constructive impulses of all who work and upon its ability to arouse and continue interest in the necessary activities. 14._____
    A. develop   B. efficiency   C. state   D. inspiration

15. The selection of managers on the basis of technical knowledge alone seems to recognize that the essential characteristic of management is getting things done through others, thereby demanding skills that are essential in coordinating the activities of subordinates. 15._____
    A. training   B. fails
    C. organization   D. improving

16. Only when it is deliberate and when it is clearly understood what impressions the ease of communication will probably create in the minds of employees and subordinate management, should top management refrain from commenting on a subject that is of general concern. 16._____
    A. obvious   B. benefit   C. doubt   D. absence

17. Scientific planning of work requires careful analysis of facts and a precise plan of action for the whims and fancies of executives that often provide only a vague indication of work to be done. 17._____
    A. substitutes   B. development
    C. preliminary   D. comprehensive

18. Assume that you are a supervisor. One of the workers under your supervision is careless about the routine aspects of his work. 18._____
    Of the following, the action MOST likely to develop in this worker a better attitude toward job routines is to demonstrate that
    A. it is just as easy to do his job the right way
    B. organization of his job will leave more time for field work
    C. the routine part of the job is essential to performing a good piece of work
    D. job routines are a responsibility of the worker

19. A supervisor can MOST effectively secure necessary improvement in a worker's office work by
    A. encouraging the worker to keep abreast of his work
    B. relating the routine part of his job to the total job to be done
    C. helping the worker to establish a good system for covering his office work and holding him to it
    D. informing the worker that he will be required to organize his work more efficiently

20. A supervisor should offer criticism in such a manner that the criticisms is helpful and not overwhelming.
    Of the following, the LEAST valid inference that can be drawn on the basis of the above statement is that a supervisor should
    A. demonstrate that the criticism is partial and not total
    B. give criticism in such a way that it does not undermine the worker's self-confidence
    C. keep his relationships with the worker objective
    D. keep criticism directed towards general work performance

21. The one of the following areas in which a worker may LEAST reasonably expect direct assistance from the supervisor is in
    A. building up rapport with all clients
    B. gaining insight into the unmet needs of clients
    C. developing an understanding of community resources
    D. interpreting agency policies and procedures

22. You are informed that a worker under your supervision has submitted a letter complaining of unfair service rating.
    Of the following, the MOST valid assumption for you to make concerning this worker is that he should be
    A. more adequately supervised in the future
    B. called in for a supervisory conference
    C. given a transfer to some other unit where he may be more happy
    D. given no more consideration than any other inefficient worker

23. Assume that you are a supervisor. You find that a somewhat bewildered worker, newly appointed to the department, hesitates to ask questions for fear of showing his ignorance and jeopardizing his position.
    Of the following, the BEST procedure for you to follow is to
    A. try to discover the reason for his evident fear of authority
    B. tell him that when he is in doubt about a procedure or a policy he should consult his fellow workers
    C. develop with the worker a plan for more frequent supervisory conferences
    D. explain why each staff member is eager to give him available information that will help him do a good job

24. Of the following, the MOST effective method of helping a newly-appointed employee adjust to his new job is to
    A. assure him that with experience his uncertain attitudes will be replaced by a professional approach
    B. help him, by accepting him as he is, to have confidence in his ability to handle the job
    C. help him to be on guard against the development of punitive attitudes
    D. help him to recognize the mutability of the agency's policies and procedures

25. Suppose that, as a supervisor, you have scheduled an individual conference with an experienced employee under your supervision.
    Of the following, the BEST plan of action for this conference is to
    A. discuss the work that the employee is most interested in
    B. plan with the employee to cover any problems that are difficult for him
    C. advise the employee that the conference is his to do with as he sees fit
    D. spot check the employee's work in advance and select those areas for discussion in which the employee has done poor work

26. Of the following, the CHIEF function of a supervisor should be to
    A. assist in the planning of new policies and the evaluation of existing ones
    B. promote congenial relationships among members of the staff
    C. achieve optimum functioning of each unit and each worker
    D. promote the smooth functioning of job routines

27. The competent supervisor must realize the importance of planning.
    Of the following, the aspect of planning which is LEAST appropriately considered a responsibility of the supervisor is
    A. long-range planning for the proper functioning of his unit
    B. planning to take care of peak and slack periods
    C. planning to cover agency policies in group conferences
    D. long-range planning to develop community resources

28. The one of the following objectives which should be of LEAST concern to the supervisor in the performance of his duties is to
    A. help the worker to make friends with all of his fellow employees
    B. be impartial and fair to all members of the staff
    C. stimulate the worker's growth on the job
    D. meet the needs of the individual employee

29. The one of the following which is LEAST properly considered a direct responsibility of the supervisor is
    A. liaison between the staff and the administrator
    B. interpreting administrative orders and procedures to the employees
    C. training new employees
    D. maintaining staff morale at a high level

30. In order to teach the employee to develop an objective approach, the BEST action for the supervisor to take is to help the worker to
    A. develop a sincere interest in his job
    B. understand the varied responsibilities that are an integral part of his job
    C. differentiate clearly between himself as a friend and as an employee
    D. find satisfaction in his work

31. If the employee shows excessive submission which indicates a need for dependence on the supervisor in handling an assignment, it would be MOST advisable for the supervisor to
    A. indicate firmly that the employee-supervisor relationship does not call for submission
    B. define areas of responsibility of employee and supervisor
    C. recognize the employee's need and of supervisor
    D. recognize the employee's need to be sustained and supported and help him by making decisions for him

32. Assume that, as a supervisor, you are conducting a group conference.
    Of the following, the BEST procedure for you to follow in order to stimulate group discussion is to
    A. permit the active participation of all members
    B. direct the discussion to an acceptable conclusion
    C. resolve conflicts of opinion among members of the group
    D. present a question for discussion on which the group members have some knowledge or experience

33. Suppose that, as a new supervisor, you wish to inform the staff under your supervision of your methods of operation.
    Of the following, the BEST procedure for you to follow is to
    A. advise the staff that they will learn gradually from experience
    B. inform each employee in an individual conference
    C. call a group conference for this purpose
    D. distribute a written memorandum among all members of the staff

34. The MOST constructive and effective method of correcting an employee who has made a mistake is, in general, to
    A. explain that his evaluation is related to his errors
    B. point out immediately where he erred and tell him how it should have been done
    C. show him how to readjust his methods so as to avoid similar errors in the future
    D. try to discover by an indirect method why the error was made

35. The MOST effective method for the supervisor to follow in order to obtain the cooperation of an employee under his supervision is, wherever possible, to
    A. maintain a careful record of performance in order to keep the employee on his toes
    B. give the employee recognition in order to promote greater effort and give him more satisfaction in his work

C. try to gain the employee's cooperation for the good of the service
D. advise the employee that his advancement on the job depends on his cooperation

36. Of the following, the MOST appropriate initial course for an employee to take when he is unable to clarify a policy with his supervisor is to
    A. bring up the problem at the next group conference
    B. discuss the policy immediately with his fellow employees
    C. accept the supervisor's interpretation as final
    D. determine what responsibility he has for putting the policy into effect

37. Good administration allows for different treatment of different workers. Of the following, the CHIEF implication of this statement is that
    A. it would be unfair for the supervisor not to treat all staff members alike
    B. fear of favoritism tends to undermine staff morale
    C. best results are obtained by individualization within the limits of fair treatment
    D. difficult problems call for a different kind of approach

38. The MOST effective and appropriate method of building efficiency and morale in a group of employees is, in general,
    A. by stressing the economic motive
    B. through use of the authority inherent in the position
    C. by a friendly approach to all
    D. by a discipline that is fair but strict

39. Of the following, the LEAST valid basis for the assignment of work to an employee is the
    A. kind of service to be rendered
    B. experience and training of the employee
    C. health and capacity of the employee
    D. racial composition of the community where the office is located

40. The CHIEF justification for staff education, consisting of in-service training, lies in its contribution to
    A. improvement in the quality of work performed
    B. recruitment of a better type of employee
    C. employee morale, accruing from a feeling of growth on the job
    D. the satisfaction that the employee gets on his job

41. Suppose that you are a supervisor. An employee no longer with your department requests you, as his former supervisor, to write a letter recommending him for a position with a private organization.
    Of the following the BEST procedure for you to follow is to include in the letter only information that
    A. will help the applicant get the job
    B. is clear, factual, and substantiated
    C. is known to you personally
    D. can readily be corroborated by personal interview

42. Of the following, the MOST important item on which to base the efficiency evaluation of an employee under your supervision is
    A. the nature of the relationship that he has built up with his fellow employees
    B. how he gets along with his supervisors
    C. his personal habits and skills
    D. the effectiveness of his control over his work

43. According to generally accepted personnel practice, the MOST effective method of building morale in a new employee is to
    A. exercise caution in praising the employee, lest he become overconfident
    B. give sincere and frank recommendation whenever possible in order to stimulate interest and effort
    C. praise the employee highly even for mediocre performance so that he will be stimulated to do better
    D. warn the employee frequently that he cannot hope to succeed unless he puts forth his best efforts

44. Errors made by newly-appointed employees often follow a predictable pattern. The one of the following errors likely to have LEAST serious consequences is the tendency of a new employee to
    A. discuss problems that are outside his province with the client
    B. persuade the client to accept the worker's solution of a problem
    C. be two strict in carrying out departmental policy and procedure
    D. depend upon the use of authority due to his inexperience and lack of skill in working with people

45. The MOST effective way for a supervisor to break down a worker's defensive stand against supervisory guidance is to
    A. come to an understanding with him on the mutual responsibilities involved in the job of the employee and that of the supervisor
    B. tell him he must feel free to express his opinions and to discuss basic problems
    C. show him how to develop toward greater objectivity, sensitivity, and understanding
    D. advise him that it is necessary to carry out agency policy and procedures in order to do a good job

46. Of the following, the LEAST essential function of the supervisor who is conducting a group conference should be to
    A. keep attention focused on the purpose of the conference
    B. encourage discussion of controversial points
    C. make certain that all possible viewpoints are discussed
    D. be thoroughly prepared in advance

47. When conducting a group conference, the supervisor should be LEAST concerned with
    A. providing an opportunity for the free interchange of ideas
    B. imparting knowledge and understanding of the work

C. leading the discussion toward a planned goal
D. pointing out where individual workers have erred in work practice

48. If the participants in a group conference are unable to agree on the proper application of a concept to the work of a department, the MOST suitable temporary procedure for the supervisor to follow is to
   A. suggest that each member think the subject through before the next meeting
   B. tell the group to examine their differences for possible conflicts with present policies
   C. suggest that practices can be changed because of new conditions
   D. state the acceptable practice in the agency and whether deviations from such practice can be permitted

49. If an employee is to participate constructively in any group discussion, it is MOST important that he have
   A. advance notice of the agenda for the meeting
   B. long experience in the department
   C. knowledge and experience in the particular work
   D. the ability to assume a leadership role

50. Of the following, the MOST important principle for the supervisor to follow when conducting a group discussion is that he should
   A. move the discussion toward acceptance by the group of a particular point of view
   B. express his ideas clearly and succinctly
   C. lead the group to accept the authority inherent in his position
   D. contribute to the discussion from his knowledge and experience

KEY (CORRECT ANSWERS)

1.	B	11.	C	21.	A	31.	B	41.	B
2.	C	12.	B	22.	B	32.	D	42.	D
3.	B	13.	B	23.	C	33.	C	43.	B
4.	D	14.	C	24.	B	34.	C	44.	C
5.	A	15.	B	25.	B	35.	B	45.	A
6.	B	16.	D	26.	C	36.	D	46.	B
7.	A	17.	A	27.	D	37.	C	47.	D
8.	A	18.	D	28.	A	38.	D	48.	D
9.	D	19.	B	29.	A	39.	D	49.	A
10.	D	20.	D	30.	C	40.	A	50.	D

PHILOSOPHY, PRINCIPLES, PRACTICES, AND TECHNICS OF SUPERVISION, ADMINISTRATION, MANAGEMENT, AND ORGANIZATION

TABLE OF CONTENTS

	Page
MEANING OF SUPERVISION	1
THE OLD AND THE NEW SUPERVISION	1
THE EIGHT (8) BASIC PRINCIPLES OF THE NEW SUPERVISION	1
I. Principle of Responsibility	1
II. Principle of Authority	2
III. Principle of Self-Growth	2
IV. Principle of Individual Worth	2
V. Principle of Creative Leadership	2
VI. Principle of Success and Failure	2
VII. Principle of Science	3
VIII. Principle of Cooperation	3
WHAT IS ADMINISTRATION?	3
I. Practices Commonly Classed as "Supervisory"	3
II. Practices Commonly Classed as "Administrative"	3
III. Practices Commonly Classed as Both "Supervisory" and "Administrative"	4
RESPONSIBILITIES OF THE SUPERVISOR	4
COMPETENCIES OF THE SUPERVISOR	4
THE PROFESSIONAL SUPERVISOR-EMPLOYEE RELATIONSHIP	4
MINI-TEXT IN SUPERVISION, ADMINISTRATION, MANAGEMENT, AND ORGANIZATION	5
I. Brief Highlights	5
A. Levels of Management	6
B. What the Supervisor Must Learn	6
C. A Definition of Supervision	6
D. Elements of the Team Concept	6
E. Principles of Organization	6
F. The Four Important Parts of Every Job	7
G. Principles of Delegation	7
H. Principles of Effective Communications	7
I. Principles of Work Improvement	7
J. Areas of Job Improvement	7
K. Seven Key Points in Making Improvements	8

	L.	Corrective Techniques for Job Improvement	8
	M.	A Planning Checklist	8
	N.	Five Characteristics of Good Directions	9
	O.	Types of Directions	9
	P.	Controls	9
	Q.	Orienting the New Employee	9
	R.	Checklist for Orienting New Employees	9
	S.	Principles of Learning	10
	T.	Causes of Poor Performance	10
	U.	Four Major Steps in On-the-Job Instructions	10
	V.	Employees Want Five Things	10
	W.	Some Don'ts in Regard to Praise	11
	X.	How to Gain Your Workers' Confidence	11
	Y.	Sources of Employee Problems	11
	Z.	The Supervisor's Key to Discipline	11
	AA.	Five Important Processes of Management	12
	BB.	When the Supervisor Fails to Plan	12
	CC.	Fourteen General Principles of Management	12
	DD.	Change	12
II.	Brief Topical Summaries		13
	A.	Who/What is the Supervisor?	13
	B.	The Sociology of Work	13
	C.	Principles and Practices of Supervision	14
	D.	Dynamic Leadership	14
	E.	Processes for Solving Problems	15
	F.	Training for Results	15
	G.	Health, Safety, and Accident Prevention	16
	H.	Equal Employment Opportunity	16
	I.	Improving Communications	16
	J.	Self-Development	17
	K.	Teaching and Training	17
		1. The Teaching Process	17
		a. Preparation	17
		b. Presentation	18
		c. Summary	18
		d. Application	18
		e. Evaluation	18
		2. Teaching Methods	18
		a. Lecture	18
		b. Discussion	18
		c. Demonstration	19
		d. Performance	19
		e. Which Method to Use	19

PHILOSOPHY, PRINCIPLES, PRACTICES, AND TECHNICS OF SUPERVISION, ADMINISTRATION, MANAGEMENT, AND ORGANIZATION

MEANING OF SUPERVISION

The extension of the democratic philosophy has been accompanied by an extension in the scope of supervision. Modern leaders and supervisors no longer think of supervision in the narrow sense of being confined chiefly to visiting employees, supplying materials, or rating the staff. They regard supervision as being intimately related to all the concerned agencies of society, they speak of the supervisor's function in terms of "growth," rather than the "improvement" of employees.

This modern concept of supervision may be defined as follows: Supervision is leadership and the development of leadership within groups which are cooperatively engaged in inspection, research, training, guidance, and evaluation.

THE OLD AND THE NEW SUPERVISION

TRADITIONAL
1. Inspection
2. Focused on the employee
3. Visitation
4. Random and haphazard
5. Imposed and authoritarian
6. One person usually

MODERN
1. Study and analysis
2. Focused on aims, materials, methods, supervisors, employees, environment
3. Demonstrations, intervisitation, workshops, directed reading, bulletins, etc.
4. Definitely organized and planned (scientific)
5. Cooperative and democratic
6. Many persons involved (creative)

THE EIGHT (8) BASIC PRINCIPLES OF THE NEW SUPERVISION

I. Principle of Responsibility
   Authority to act and responsibility for acting must be joined.
   A. If you give responsibility, give authority.
   B. Define employee duties clearly.
   C. Protect employees from criticism by others.
   D. Recognize the rights as well as obligations of employees.
   E. Achieve the aims of a democratic society insofar as it is possible within the area of your work.
   F. Establish a situation favorable to training and learning.
   G. Accept ultimate responsibility for everything done in your section, unit, office, division, department.
   H. Good administration and good supervision are inseparable.

II. Principle of Authority
The success of the supervisor is measured by the extent to which the power of authority is not used.
- A. Exercise simplicity and informality in supervision
- B. Use the simplest machinery of supervision
- C. If it is good for the organization as a whole, it is probably justified.
- D. Seldom be arbitrary or authoritative.
- E. Do not base your work on the power of position or of personality.
- F. Permit and encourage the free expression of opinions.

III. Principle of Self-Growth
The success of the supervisor is measured by the extent to which, and the speed with which, he is no longer needed.
- A. Base criticism on principles, not on specifics.
- B. Point out higher activities to employees.
- C. Train for self-thinking by employees to meet new situations.
- D. Stimulate initiative, self-reliance, and individual responsibility
- E. Concentrate on stimulating the growth of employees rather than on removing defects.

IV. Principle of Individual Worth
Respect for the individual is a paramount consideration in supervision.
- A. Be human and sympathetic in dealing with employees.
- B. Don't nag about things to be done.
- C. Recognize the individual differences among employees and seek opportunities to permit best expression of each personality.

V. Principle of Creative Leadership
The best supervision is that which is not apparent to the employee.
- A. Stimulate, don't drive employees to creative action.
- B. Emphasize doing good things.
- C. Encourage employees to do what they do best.
- D. Do not be too greatly concerned with details of subject or method.
- E. Do not be concerned exclusively with immediate problems and activities.
- F. Reveal higher activities and make them both desired and maximally possible.
- G. Determine procedures in the light of each situation but see that these are derived from a sound basic philosophy.
- H. Aid, inspire, and lead so as to liberate the creative spirit latent in all good employees.

VI. Principle of Success and Failure
There are no unsuccessful employees, only unsuccessful supervisors who have failed to give proper leadership.
- A. Adapt suggestions to the capacities, attitudes, and prejudices of employees.
- B. Be gradual, be progressive, be persistent.
- C. Help the employee find the general principle; have the employee apply his own problem to the general principle.
- D. Give adequate appreciation for good work and honest effort.
- E. Anticipate employee difficulties and help to prevent them.
- F. Encourage employees to do the desirable things they will do anyway.
- G. Judge your supervision by the results it secures.

VII. Principle of Science
Successful supervision is scientific, objective, and experimental. It is based on facts, not on prejudices.
  A. Be cumulative in results.
  B. Never divorce your suggestions from the goals of training.
  C. Don't be impatient of results.
  D. Keep all matters on a professional, not a personal, level.
  E. Do not be concerned exclusively with immediate problems and activities.
  F. Use objective means of determining achievement and rating where possible.

VIII. Principle of Cooperation
Supervision is a cooperative enterprise between supervisor and employee.
  A. Begin with conditions as they are.
  B. Ask opinions of all involved when formulating policies.
  C. Organization is as good as its weakest link.
  D. Let employees help to determine policies and department programs.
  E. Be approachable and accessible—physically and mentally.
  F. Develop pleasant social relationships.

WHAT IS ADMINISTRATION

Administration is concerned with providing the environment, the material facilities, and the operational procedures that will promote the maximum growth and development of supervisors and employees. (Organization is an aspect and a concomitant of administration.)

There is no sharp line of demarcation between supervision and administration; these functions are intimately interrelated and, often, overlapping. They are complementary activities.

I. Practices Commonly Classed as "Supervisory"
  A. Conducting employees' conferences
  B. Visiting sections, units, offices, divisions, departments
  C. Arranging for demonstrations
  D. Examining plans
  E. Suggesting professional reading
  F. Interpreting bulletins
  G. Recommending in-service training courses
  H. Encouraging experimentation
  I. Appraising employee morale
  J. Providing for intervisitation

II. Practices Commonly Classified as "Administrative"
  A. Management of the office
  B. Arrangement of schedules for extra duties
  C. Assignment of rooms or areas
  D. Distribution of supplies
  E. Keeping records and reports
  F. Care of audio-visual materials
  G. Keeping inventory records
  H. Checking record cards and books

    I.   Programming special activities
    J.   Checking on the attendance and punctuality of employees

III. Practices Commonly Classified as Both "Supervisory" and "Administrative"
    A. Program construction
    B. Testing or evaluating outcomes
    C. Personnel accounting
    D. Ordering instructional materials

RESPONSIBILITIES OF THE SUPERVISOR

A person employed in a supervisory capacity must constantly be able to improve his own efficiency and ability. He represent the employer to the employees and only continuous self-examination can make him a capable supervisor.

Leadership and training are the supervisor's responsibility. An efficient working unit is one in which the employees work with the supervisor. It is his job to bring out the best in his employees. He must always be relaxed, courteous, and calm in his association with his employees. Their feelings are important, and a harsh attitude does not develop the most efficient employees.

COMPETENCES OF THE SUPERVISOR

    I.   Complete knowledge of the duties and responsibilities of his position.
    II.   To be able to organize a job, plan ahead, and carry through.
    III.   To have self-confidence and initiative.
    IV.   To be able to handle the unexpected situation and make quick decisions.
    V.   To be able to properly train subordinates in the positions they are best suited for.
    VI.   To be able to keep good human relations among his subordinates.
    VII. To be able to keep good human relations between his subordinates and himself and to earn their respect and trust.

THE PROFESSIONAL SUPERVISOR-EMPLOYEE RELATIONSHIP

There are two kinds of efficiency: one kind is only apparent and is produced in organizations through the exercise of mere discipline; this is but a simulation of the second, or true, efficiency which springs from spontaneous cooperation. If you are a manager, no matter how great or small your responsibility, it is your job, in the final analysis, to create and develop this involuntary cooperation among the people whom you supervise. For, no matter how powerful a combination of money, machines, and materials a company may have, this is a dead and sterile thing without a team of willing, thinking, and articulate people to guide it.

The following 21 points are presented as indicative of the exemplary basic relationship that should exist between supervisor and employee:

1. Each person wants to be liked and respected by his fellow employee and wants to be treated with consideration and respect by his superior.
2. The most competent employee will make an error. However, in a unit where good relations exist between the supervisor and his employees, tenseness and fear do not exist. Thus, errors are not hidden or covered up, and the efficiency of a unit is not impaired.

3. Subordinates resent rules, regulations, or orders that are unreasonable or unexplained.
4. Subordinates are quick to resent unfairness, harshness, injustices, and favoritism.
5. An employee will accept responsibility if he knows that he will be complimented for a job well done, and not too harshly chastised for failure; that his supervisor will check the cause of the failure, and, if it was the supervisor's fault, he will assume the blame therefore. If it was the employee's fault, his supervisor will explain the correct method or means of handling the responsibility.
6. An employee wants to receive credit for a suggestion he has made, that is used. If a suggestion cannot be used, the employee is entitled to an explanation. The supervisor should not say "no" and close the subject.
7. Fear and worry slow up a worker's ability. Poor working environment can impair his physical and mental health. A good supervisor avoids forceful methods, threats, and arguments to get a job done.
8. A forceful supervisor is able to train his employees individually and as a team, and is able to motivate them in the proper channels.
9. A mature supervisor is able to properly evaluate his subordinates and to keep them happy and satisfied.
10. A sensitive supervisor will never patronize his subordinates.
11. A worthy supervisor will respect his employees' confidences.
12. Definite and clear-cut responsibilities should be assigned to each executive.
13. Responsibility should always be coupled with corresponding authority.
14. No change should be made in the scope or responsibilities of a position without a definite understanding to that effect on the part of all persons concerned.
15. No executive or employee, occupying a single position in the organization, should be subject to definite orders from more than one source.
16. Orders should never be given to subordinates over the head of a responsible executive. Rather than do this, the officer in question should be supplanted.
17. Criticisms of subordinates should, whoever possible, be made privately, and in no case should a subordinate be criticized in the presence of executives or employees of equal or lower rank.
18. No dispute or difference between executives or employees as to authority or responsibilities should be considered too trivial for prompt and careful adjudication.
19. Promotions, wage changes, and disciplinary action should always be approved by the executive immediately superior to the one directly responsible.
20. No executive or employee should ever be required, or expected, to be at the same time an assistant to, and critic of, another.
21. Any executive whose work is subject to regular inspection should, wherever practicable, be given the assistance and facilities necessary to enable him to maintain an independent check of the quality of his work.

MINI-TEXT IN SUPERVISION, ADMINISTRATION, MANAGEMENT, AND ORGANIZATION

I. Brief Highlights

Listed concisely and sequentially are major headings and important data in the field for quick recall and review.

A. Levels of Management
Any organization of some size has several levels of management. In terms of a ladder, the levels are:

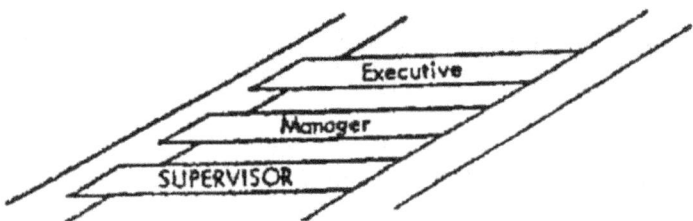

The first level is very important because it is the beginning point of management leadership.

B. What the Supervisor Must Learn
A supervisor must learn to:
1. Deal with people and their differences
2. Get the job done through people
3. Recognize the problems when they exist
4. Overcome obstacles to good performance
5. Evaluate the performance of people
6. Check his own performance in terms of accomplishment

C. A Definition of Supervisor
The term supervisor means any individual having authority, in the interests of the employer, to hire, transfer, suspend, lay-off, recall, promote, discharge, assign, reward, or discipline other employees or responsibility to direct them, or to adjust their grievances, or effectively to recommend such action, if, in connection with the foregoing, exercise of such authority is not of a merely routine or clerical nature but requires the use of independent judgment.

D. Elements of the Team Concept
What is involved in teamwork? The component parts are:
1. Members
2. A leader
3. Goals
4. Plans
5. Cooperation
6. Spirit

E. Principles of Organization
1. A team member must know what his job is.
2. Be sure that the nature and scope of a job are understood.
3. Authority and responsibility should be carefully spelled out.
4. A supervisor should be permitted to make the maximum number of decisions affecting his employees.
5. Employees should report to only one supervisor.
6. A supervisor should direct only as many employees as he can handle effectively.
7. An organization plan should be flexible.

8. Inspection and performance of work should be separate.
9. Organizational problems should receive immediate attention.
10. Assign work in line with ability and experience.

F. The Four Important Parts of Every Job
1. Inherent in every job is the *accountability* for results.
2. A second set of factors in every job is *responsibilities*.
3. Along with duties and responsibilities one must have the *authority* to act within certain limits without obtaining permission to proceed.
4. No job exists in a vacuum. The supervisor is surrounded by key *relationships*.

G. Principles of Delegation
Where work is delegated for the first time, the supervisor should think in terms of these questions:
1. Who is best qualified to do this?
2. Can an employee improve his abilities by doing this?
3. How long should an employee spend on this?
4. Are there any special problems for which he will need guidance?
5. How broad a delegation can I make?

H. Principles of Effective Communications
1. Determine the media.
2. To whom directed?
3. Identification and source authority.
4. Is communication understood?

I. Principles of Work Improvement
1. Most people usually do only the work which is assigned to them.
2. Workers are likely to fit assigned work into the time available to perform it.
3. A good workload usually stimulates output.
4. People usually do their best work when they know that results will be reviewed or inspected.
5. Employees usually feel that someone else is responsible for conditions of work, workplace layout, job methods, type of tools/equipment, and other such factors.
6. Employees are usually defensive about their job security.
7. Employees have natural resistance to change.
8. Employees can support or destroy a supervisor.
9. A supervisor usually earns the respect of his people through his personal example of diligence and efficiency.

J. Areas of Job Improvement
The areas of job improvement are quite numerous, but the most common ones which a supervisor can identify and utilize are:
1. Departmental layout
2. Flow of work
3. Workplace layout
4. Utilization of manpower
5. Work methods
6. Materials handling

7. Utilization
8. Motion economy

K. Seven Key Points in Making Improvements
1. Select the job to be improved
2. Study how it is being done now
3. Question the present method
4. Determine actions to be taken
5. Chart proposed method
6. Get approval and apply
7. Solicit worker participation

L. Corrective Techniques of Job Improvement
Specific Problems
1. Size of workload
2. Inability to meet schedules
3. Strain and fatigue
4. Improper use of men and skills
5. Waste, poor quality, unsafe conditions
6. Bottleneck conditions that hinder output
7. Poor utilization of equipment and machine
8. Efficiency and productivity of labor

General Improvement
1. Departmental layout
2. Flow of work
3. Work plan layout
4. Utilization of manpower
5. Work methods
6. Materials handling
7. Utilization of equipment
8. Motion economy

Corrective Techniques
1. Study with scale model
2. Flow chart study
3. Motion analysis
4. Comparison of units produced to standard allowance
5. Methods analysis
6. Flow chart and equipment study
7. Down time vs. running time
8. Motion analysis

M. A Planning Checklist
1. Objectives
2. Controls
3. Delegations
4. Communications
5. Resources
6. Manpower

7. Equipment
8. Supplies and materials
9. Utilization of time
10. Safety
11. Money
12. Work
13. Timing of improvements

N. Five Characteristics of Good Directions
In order to get results, directions must be:
1. Possible of accomplishment
2. Agreeable with worker interests
3. Related to mission
4. Planned and complete
5. Unmistakably clear

O. Types of Directions
1. Demands or direct orders
2. Requests
3. Suggestion or implication
4. volunteering

P. Controls
A typical listing of the overall areas in which the supervisor should establish controls might be:
1. Manpower
2. Materials
3. Quality of work
4. Quantity of work
5. Time
6. Space
7. Money
8. Methods

Q. Orienting the New Employee
1. Prepare for him
2. Welcome the new employee
3. Orientation for the job
4. Follow-up

R. Checklist for Orienting New Employees   Yes   No
1. Do you appreciate the feelings of new employees when they first report for work?   ___   ___
2. Are you aware of the fact that the new employee must make a big adjustment to his job?   ___   ___
3. Have you given him good reasons for liking the job and the organization?   ___   ___
4. Have you prepared for his first day on the job?   ___   ___
5. Did you welcome him cordially and make him feel needed?   ___   ___

	Yes	No

6. Did you establish rapport with him so that he feels free to talk and discuss matters with you? ___ ___
7. Did you explain his job to him and his relationship to you? ___ ___
8. Does he know that his work will be evaluated periodically on a basis that is fair and objective? ___ ___
9. Did you introduce him to his fellow workers in such a way that they are likely to accept him? ___ ___
10. Does he know what employee benefits he will receive? ___ ___
11. Does he understand the importance of being on the job and what to do if he must leave his duty station? ___ ___
12. Has he been impressed with the importance of accident prevention and safe practice? ___ ___
13. Does he generally know his way around the department? ___ ___
14. Is he under the guidance of a sponsor who will teach the right way of doing things? ___ ___
15. Do you plan to follow-up so that he will continue to adjust successfully to his job? ___ ___

S. Principles of Learning
   1. Motivation
   2. Demonstration or explanation
   3. Practice

T. Causes of Poor Performance
   1. Improper training for job
   2. Wrong tools
   3. Inadequate directions
   4. Lack of supervisory follow-up
   5. Poor communications
   6. Lack of standards of performance
   7. Wrong work habits
   8. Low morale
   9. Other

U. Four Major Steps in On-The-Job Instruction
   1. Prepare the worker
   2. Present the operation
   3. Tryout performance
   4. Follow-up

V. Employees Want Five Things
   1. Security
   2. Opportunity
   3. Recognition
   4. Inclusion
   5. Expression

W. Some Don'ts in Regard to Praise
   1. Don't praise a person for something he hasn't done.
   2. Don't praise a person unless you can be sincere.
   3. Don't be sparing in praise just because your superior withholds it from you.
   4. Don't let too much time elapse between good performance and recognition of it

X. How to Gain Your Workers' Confidence
   Methods of developing confidence include such things as:
   1. Knowing the interests, habits, hobbies of employees
   2. Admitting your own inadequacies
   3. Sharing and telling of confidence in others
   4. Supporting people when they are in trouble
   5. Delegating matters that can be well handled
   6. Being frank and straightforward about problems and working conditions
   7. Encouraging others to bring their problems to you
   8. Taking action on problems which impede worker progress

Y. Sources of Employee Problems
   On-the-job causes might be such things as:
   1. A feeling that favoritism is exercised in assignments
   2. Assignment of overtime
   3. An undue amount of supervision
   4. Changing methods or systems
   5. Stealing of ideas or trade secrets
   6. Lack of interest in job
   7. Threat of reduction in force
   8. Ignorance or lack of communications
   9. Poor equipment
   10. Lack of knowing how supervisor feels toward employee
   11. Shift assignments

   Off-the-job problems might have to do with:
   1. Health
   2. Finances
   3. Housing
   4. Family

Z. The Supervisor's Key to Discipline
   There are several key points about discipline which the supervisor should keep in mind:
   1. Job discipline is one of the disciplines of life and is directed by the supervisor.
   2. It is more important to correct an employee fault than to fix blame for it.
   3. Employee performance is affected by problems both on the job and off.
   4. Sudden or abrupt changes in behavior can be indications of important employee problems.
   5. Problems should be dealt with as soon as possible after they are identified.
   6. The attitude of the supervisor may have more to do with solving problems than the techniques of problem solving.
   7. Correction of employee behavior should be resorted to only after the supervisor is sure that training or counseling will not be helpful.

8. Be sure to document your disciplinary actions.
9. Make sure that you are disciplining on the basis of facts rather than personal feelings.
10. Take each disciplinary step in order, being careful not to make snap judgments, or decisions based on impatience.

AA. Five Important Processes of Management
1. Planning
2. Organizing
3. Scheduling
4. Controlling
5. Motivating

BB. When the Supervisor Fails to Plan
1. Supervisor creates impression of not knowing his job
2. May lead to excessive overtime
3. Job runs itself—supervisor lacks control
4. Deadlines and appointments missed
5. Parts of the work go undone
6. Work interrupted by emergencies
7. Sets a bad example
8. Uneven workload creates peaks and valleys
9. Too much time on minor details at expense of more important tasks

CC. Fourteen General Principles of Management
1. Division of work
2. Authority and responsibility
3. Discipline
4. Unity of command
5. Unity of direction
6. Subordination of individual interest to general interest
7. Remuneration of personnel
8. Centralization
9. Scalar chain
10. Order
11. Equity
12. Stability of tenure of personnel
13. Initiative
14. Esprit de corps

DD. Change

Bringing about change is perhaps attempted more often, and yet less well understood, than anything else the supervisor does. How do people generally react to change? (People tend to resist change that is imposed upon them by other individuals or circumstances.

Change is characteristic of every situation. It is a part of every real endeavor where the efforts of people are concerned.

1. Why do people resist change?
   People may resist change because of:
   a. Fear of the unknown
   b. Implied criticism
   c. Unpleasant experiences in the past
   d. Fear of loss of status
   e. Threat to the ego
   f. Fear of loss of economic stability

2. How can we best overcome the resistance to change?
   In initiating change, take these steps:
   a. Get ready to sell
   b. Identify sources of help
   c. Anticipate objections
   d. Sell benefits
   e. Listen in depth
   f. Follow up

II. Brief Topical Summaries

   A. Who/What is the Supervisor?
      1. The supervisor is often called the "highest level employee and the lowest level manager."
      2. A supervisor is a member of both management and the work group. He acts as a bridge between the two.
      3. Most problems in supervision are in the area of human relations, or people problems.
      4. Employees expect: Respect, opportunity to learn and to advance, and a sense of belonging, and so forth.
      5. Supervisors are responsible for directing people and organizing work. Planning is of paramount importance.
      6. A position description is a set of duties and responsibilities inherent to a given position.
      7. It is important to keep the position description up-to-date and to provide each employee with his own copy.

   B. The Sociology of Work
      1. People are alike in many ways; however, each individual is unique.
      2. The supervisor is challenged in getting to know employee differences. Acquiring skills in evaluating individuals is an asset.
      3. Maintaining meaningful working relationships in the organization is of great importance.
      4. The supervisor has an obligation to help individuals to develop to their fullest potential.
      5. Job rotation on a planned basis helps to build versatility and to maintain interest and enthusiasm in work groups.
      6. Cross training (job rotation) provides backup skills.

7. The supervisor can help reduce tension by maintaining a sense of humor, providing guidance to employees, and by making reasonable and timely decisions. Employees respond favorably to working under reasonably predictable circumstances.
8. Change is characteristic of all managerial behavior. The supervisor must adjust to changes in procedures, new methods, technological changes, and to a number of new and sometimes challenging situations.
9. To overcome the natural tendency for people to resist change, the supervisor should become more skillful in initiating change.

C. Principles and Practices of Supervision
1. Employees should be required to answer to only one superior.
2. A supervisor can effectively direct only a limited number of employees, depending upon the complexity, variety, and proximity of the jobs involved.
3. The organizational chart presents the organization in graphic form. It reflects lines of authority and responsibility as well as interrelationships of units within the organization.
4. Distribution of work can be improved through an analysis using the "Work Distribution Chart."
5. The "Work Distribution Chart" reflects the division of work within a unit in understandable form.
6. When related tasks are given to an employee, he has a better chance of increasing his skills through training.
7. The individual who is given the responsibility for tasks must also be given the appropriate authority to insure adequate results.
8. The supervisor should delegate repetitive, routine work. Preparation of recurring reports, maintaining leave and attendance records are some examples.
9. Good discipline is essential to good task performance. Discipline is reflected in the actions of employees on the job in the absence of supervision.
10. Disciplinary action may have to be taken when the positive aspects of discipline have failed. Reprimand, warning, and suspension are examples of disciplinary action.
11. If a situation calls for a reprimand, be sure it is deserved and remember it is to be done in private.

D. Dynamic Leadership
1. A style is a personal method or manner of exerting influence.
2. Authoritarian leaders often see themselves as the source of power and authority.
3. The democratic leader often perceives the group as the source of authority and power.
4. Supervisors tend to do better when using the pattern of leadership that is most natural for them.
5. Social scientists suggest that the effective supervisor use the leadership style that best fits the problem or circumstances involved.
6. All four styles—telling, selling, consulting, joining—have their place. Using one does not preclude using the other at another time.

7. The theory X point of view assumes that the average person dislikes work, will avoid it whenever possible, and must be coerced to achieve organizational objectives.
8. The theory Y point of view assumes that the average person considers work to be a natural as play, and, when the individual is committed, he requires little supervision or direction to accomplish desired objectives.
9. The leader's basic assumptions concerning human behavior and human nature affect his actions, decisions, and other managerial practices.
10. Dissatisfaction among employees is often present, but difficult to isolate. The supervisor should seek to weaken dissatisfaction by keeping promises, being sincere and considerate, keeping employees informed, and so forth.
11. Constructive suggestions should be encouraged during the natural progress of the work.

E. Processes for Solving Problems
1. People find their daily tasks more meaningful and satisfying when they can improve them.
2. The causes of problems, or the key factors, are often hidden in the background. Ability to solve problems often involves the ability to isolate them from their backgrounds. There is some substance to the cliché that some persons "can't see the forest for the trees."
3. New procedures are often developed from old ones. Problems should be broken down into manageable parts. New ideas can be adapted from old one.
4. People think differently in problem-solving situations. Using a logical, patterned approach is often useful. One approach found to be useful includes these steps:
   a. Define the problem
   b. Establish objectives
   c. Get the facts
   d. Weigh and decide
   e. Take action
   f. Evaluate action

F. Training for Results
1. Participants respond best when they feel training is important to them.
2. The supervisor has responsibility for the training and development of those who report to him.
3. When training is delegated to others, great care must be exercised to insure the trainer has knowledge, aptitude, and interest for his work as a trainer.
4. Training (learning) of some type goes on continually. The most successful supervisor makes certain the learning contributes in a productive manner to operational goals.
5. New employees are particularly susceptible to training. Older employees facing new job situations require specific training, as well as having need for development and growth opportunities.
6. Training needs require continuous monitoring.
7. The training officer of an agency is a professional with a responsibility to assist supervisors in solving training problems.

8. Many of the self-development steps important to the supervisor's own growth are equally important to the development of peers and subordinates. Knowledge of these is important when the supervisor consults with others on development and growth opportunities.

G. Health, Safety, and Accident Prevention
1. Management-minded supervisors take appropriate measures to assist employees in maintaining health and in assuring safe practices in the work environment.
2. Effective safety training and practices help to avoid injury and accidents.
3. Safety should be a management goal. All infractions of safety which are observed should be corrected without exception.
4. Employees' safety attitude, training and instruction, provision of safe tools and equipment, supervision, and leadership are considered highly important factors which contribute to safety and which can be influenced directly by supervisors.
5. When accidents do occur, they should be investigated promptly for very important reasons, including the fact that information which is gained can be used to prevent accidents in the future.

H. Equal Employment Opportunity
1. The supervisor should endeavor to treat all employees fairly, without regard to religion, race, sex, or national origin.
2. Groups tend to reflect the attitude of the leader. Prejudice can be detected even in very subtle form. Supervisors must strive to create a feeling of mutual respect and confidence in every employee.
3. Complete utilization of all human resources is a national goal. Equitable consideration should be accorded women in the work force, minority-group members, the physically and mentally handicapped, and the older employee. The important question is: "Who can do the job?"
4. Training opportunities, recognition for performance, overtime assignments, promotional opportunities, and all other personnel actions are to be handled on an equitable basis.

I. Improving Communications
1. Communications is achieving understanding between the sender and the receiver of a message. It also means sharing information—the creation of understanding.
2. Communication is basic to all human activity. Words are means of conveying meanings; however, real meanings are in people.
3. There are very practical differences in the effectiveness of one-way, impersonal, and two-way communications. Words spoken face-to-face are better understood. Telephone conversations are effective, but lack the rapport of person-to-person exchanges. The whole person communicates.
4. Cooperation and communication in an organization go hand in hand. When there is a mutual respect between people, spelling out rules and procedures for communicating is unnecessary.
5. There are several barriers to effective communications. These include failure to listen with respect and understanding, lack of skill in feedback, and misinterpreting the meanings of words used by the speaker. It is also common

practice to listen to what we want to hear, and tune out things we do not want to hear.
6. Communication is management's chief problem. The supervisor should accept the challenge to communicate more effectively and to improve interagency and intra-agency communications.
7. The supervisor may often plan for and conduct meetings. The planning phase is critical and may determine the success or the failure of a meeting.
8. Speaking before groups usually requires extra effort. Stage fright may never disappear completely, but it can be controlled.

J. Self-Development
1. Every employee is responsible for his own self-development.
2. Toastmaster and toastmistress clubs offer opportunities to improve skills in oral communications.
3. Planning for one's own self-development is of vital importance. Supervisors know their own strengths and limitations better than anyone else.
4. Many opportunities are open to aid the supervisor in his developmental efforts, including job assignments; training opportunities, both governmental and non-governmental—to include universities and professional conferences and seminars.
5. Programmed instruction offers a means of studying at one's own rate.
6. Where difficulties may arise from a supervisor's being away from his work for training, he may participate in televised home study or correspondence courses to meet his self-development needs.

K. Teaching and Training
1. The Teaching Process
Teaching is encouraging and guiding the learning activities of students toward established goals. In most cases this process consists of five steps: preparation, presentation, summarization, evaluation, and application.

   a. Preparation
   Preparation is two-fold in nature; that of the supervisor and the employee. Preparation by the supervisor is absolutely essential to success. He must know what, when, where, how, and whom he will teach. Some of the factors that should be considered are:
   1) The objectives
   2) The materials needed
   3) The methods to be used
   4) Employee participation
   5) Employee interest
   6) Training aids
   7) Evaluation
   8) Summarization

   Employee preparation consists in preparing the employee to receive the material. Probably the most important single factor in the preparation of the employee is arousing and maintaining his interest. He must know the objectives of the training, why he is there, how the material can be used, and its importance to him.

b. Presentation
   In presentation, have a carefully designed plan and follow it. The plan should be accurate and complete, yet flexible enough to meet situations as they arise. The method of presentation will be determined by the particular situation and objectives.

c. Summary
   A summary should be made at the end of every training unit and program. In addition, there may be internal summaries depending on the nature of the material being taught. The important thing is that the trainee must always be able to understand how each part of the new material relates to the whole.

d. Application
   The supervisor must arrange work so the employee will be given a chance to apply new knowledge or skills while the material is still clear in his mind and interest is high. The trainee does not really know whether he has learned the material until he has been given a chance to apply it. If the material is not applied, it loses most of its value.

e. Evaluation
   The purpose of all training is to promote learning. To determine whether the training has been a success or failure, the supervisor must evaluate this learning.
   In the broadest sense, evaluation includes all the devices, methods, skills, and techniques used by the supervisor to keep himself and the employees informed as to their progress toward the objectives they are pursuing. The extent to which the employee has mastered the knowledge, skills, and abilities, or changed his attitudes, as determined by the program objectives, is the extent to which instruction has succeeded or failed.
   Evaluation should not be confined to the end of the lesson, day, or program but should be used continuously. We shall note later the way this relates to the rest of the teaching process.

2. Teaching Methods
   A teaching method is a pattern of identifiable student and instructor activity used in presenting training material.
   All supervisors are faced with the problem of deciding which method should be used at a given time.

   a. Lecture
      The lecture is direct oral presentation of material by the supervisor. The present trend is to place less emphasis on the trainer's activity and more on that of the trainee.

   b. Discussion
      Teaching by discussion or conference involves using questions and other techniques to arouse interest and focus attention upon certain areas, and by doing so creating a learning situation. This can be one of the most

valuable methods because it gives the employees an opportunity to express their ideas and pool their knowledge.

c. Demonstration
The demonstration is used to teach how something works or how to do something. It can be used to show a principle or what the results of a series of actions will be. A well-staged demonstration is particularly effective because it shows proper methods of performance in a realistic manner.

d. Performance
Performance is one of the most fundamental of all learning techniques or teaching methods. The trainee may be able to tell how a specific operation should be performed but he cannot be sure he knows how to perform the operation until he has done so.
As with all methods, there are certain advantages and disadvantages to each method.

e. Which Method to Use
Moreover, there are other methods and techniques of teaching. It is difficult to use any method without other methods entering into it. In any learning situation, a combination of methods is usually more effective than any one method alone.

Finally, evaluation must be integrated into the other aspects of the teaching-learning process.

It must be used in the motivation of the trainees; it must be used to assist in developing understanding during the training; and it must be related to employee application of the results of training.

This is distinctly the role of the supervisor.

www.ingramcontent.com/pod-product-compliance
Lightning Source LLC
Chambersburg PA
CBHW081820300426
44116CB00014B/2431